THE MAGIC OF
FREE-MACHINE EMBROIDERY

THE MAGIC OF
FREE-MACHINE
EMBROIDERY

DOREEN CURRAN

SEARCH PRESS

Acknowledgments

My grateful thanks to members of my family who gave so generously of their own particular knowledge and expertise—Lalor, Lucinda, David, Renate, Caroline and Lynn.

I will always be thankful to Connie Hart, Vivienne Keast and all of the teachers at Dover Heights College of Technical and Further Education who gave me the beginnings of a new life.

Very special thanks to Heather Joynes and friends who gave me the support and encouragement to start this book in the first place.

In memory of my brother David Franklin, who photographed all of my work so wonderfully before he died.

Photography by David Franklin

First published in Great Britain 2001
Search Press Limited
Wellwood, North Farm Road
Tunbridge Wells, Kent, TN2 3DR

Originally published in Australia in 1992 by Kangaroo Press
An imprint of Simon & Schuster (Australia) Pty Limited
20 Barcoo Street, East Roseville NSW 2069

Reprinted 2002 and 2003

Printed in China through Colorcraft Ltd., Hong Kong

ISBN 1 903975 14 X

The publishers and author can accept no responsibility for any consequences arising from the information, advice or instructions given in this publication.

Suppliers
If you have difficulty in obtaining any of the materials and equipment mentioned in this book, then please visit the Search Press website for details of suppliers:
www.searchpress.com
Alternatively, you can write to the publishers at the address above
for a current list of stockists, including firms who offer a mail-order service.

CONTENTS

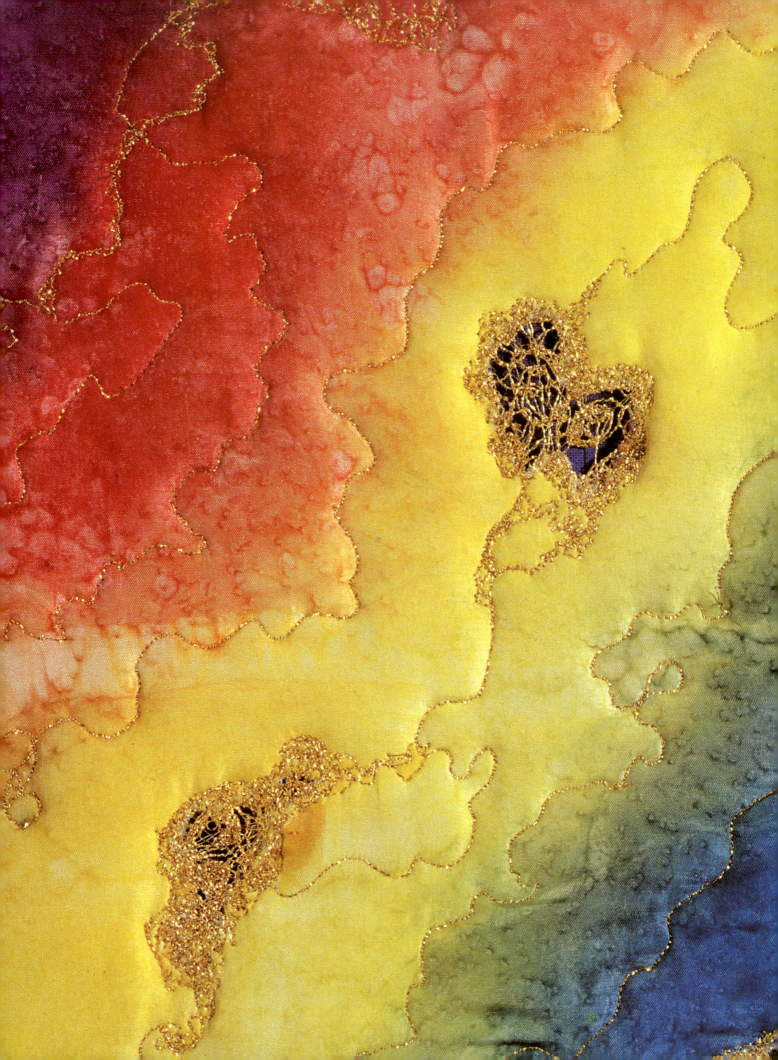

PREFACE

I have written this book on a one-to-one basis to an imaginary reader, now real, trying to explain everything in a helpful way.

Starting from the basics and leading on to the more advanced techniques of free-machine embroidery, I have included many of my own ideas to make embroidered pictures three-dimensional. I have evolved a number of building-up techniques with textures and appliqué. Thick threads, both wrapped and applied, together with stumpwork and fabric sculpting can add further dimensions. Painted backgrounds and semi-transparent layered backgrounds add to depth and mood.

I want my readers to use this book as a stepping stone to the development of their own ideas. Free-machine embroidery, being contemporary, is not tied down to traditional ways, but is a growing and liberated art. There are many avenues yet to be explored.

I dedicate this book to my readers.

Doreen Curran

1 BEGINNINGS

Free-machine embroidery is a wonderful way to embroider. It opens up a whole new world and reveals that your sewing machine has another personality.

As long as your machine can do a zig-zag stitch in addition to the ordinary straight stitch, you can use it to create many new stitches, textures and designs for yourself. You are the master, and you can guide your work in any direction you choose. With the aid of an embroidery hoop, new skills and your imagination, there is almost no limit to what you will be able to achieve.

You will need to practice, of course—every new skill requires that. Practice will bring its own rewards, and you will be delighted with the results.

With free-machine embroidery you work with a hoop, using machine tension to control the flow of the threads. You can add a variety of silky rayon threads to your existing collection of machine threads. Unusually thick threads can also be used to special effect.

This book progresses from the first basic stitches needed in an embroiderer's repertoire through to advanced free-machine embroidery techniques, which include various kinds of threadwork. I go on to stumpwork and fabric sculpting, and I have also included a chapter on painting your own backgrounds.

Each technique is described in detail, in words and photographs. Each section includes an embroidered picture which demonstrates the technique. Chapter 2, Understanding the Basics, is summarised with an easily remembered 'basic routine', followed in Chapter 3 by a chart which tells you at a glance the procedures for each particular stitch, the threads to use and the tensions to apply. An empty chart appears at the back of the book, where you can make your own notes and observations.

Another chart, in Chapter 8, is designed as a guide for creating distance, depth and dimensions. It summarises the various techniques, colours, stitches, textures and overlays you can use to make your pictures appear alive.

Many of the ideas and techniques in this book are my own inventions. I hope you will enjoy them for yourself.

Basic Requirements

The first requirement is a sewing machine, which is able to do a zig-zag stitch. It should come equipped with bobbins, accessories and an instruction book. It is important that the feed-dog can be lowered (or that there is a cover-plate to cover it).

You will need an assortment of machine needles—sizes 90/14 and 80/12 for most work—size 100/16 for the thickest fabrics or heavy embroideries. Types of needles to use are the Embroidery and Metalfil needle. Both of these have large eyes and are easier to thread.

For very tightly woven fabrics, such as pure silk, use a MicroTex needle. This has a very sharp point which penetrates the fabric cleanly. Jeans needles are also useful for their sharp point. Quilting needles are recommended for embroidering padded fabric.

Wooden embroidery hoops approximately 16 to 20 cm in diameter, 1 cm in depth, are essential items. The hoop must have an adjustment screw which can be tightened with a screwdriver. The inner ring of each hoop should be bound with bias binding to prevent your work slipping. It is worth having at least two hoops—one for practising, and the other for the actual piece. It can be especially useful to have hoops of different sizes—say, one 20 cm in diameter, the other 16 cm.

You will need a screwdriver which fits the screws on the hoops. Good quality scissors for fabric and clippers for threads are necessary.

An extra bobbin case is optional, but essential if you are serious about free-machine embroidery. The various techniques involve frequent changes of tension, so having an extra bobbin case saves time and effort.

Fabrics—any firm, closely woven cotton is good to begin with. Calico is reasonably priced and works well.

Sewing machine threads—you will be surprised how quickly you will acquire an assortment of colours in various thicknesses and fibres. Suitable cottons include Sylko, DMC 30 and DMC 50, Gütermann 50, etc. Rayons include Isafil, Madeira and Sulky, while polycotton or polyester threads include Dewhurst, Duet, Gütermann and Rasant.

Other fabrics and many other threads in various colours and thicknesses will be added as you progress.

Choosing Suitable Fabrics

As the process of free-machine embroidery places a considerable strain on the fabric being worked, care must be taken in choosing fabrics that can cope. Calico is very good to begin with, for practising and even for light-weight embroideries. Calico can be painted with fabric paints (in which case it must first be washed and pressed) and used in many other ways. It is very reasonably priced and easily obtainable. However, you won't want to use calico only, no matter how versatile it may be!

You may decide to use a coloured fabric for a particular piece. In this case choose a firm, closely woven cotton fabric for best results. If you are in any doubt about its suitability, or you find that the fabric is not as good as you first thought, try backing it with a good quality iron-on interfacing—woven or non-woven, it doesn't matter which. The interfacing helps to prevent puckering because it adds to the thickness and firmness of the fabric.

Heavy duty calico and similar thick, firm cotton fabrics are very good backgrounds both for painting and for more elaborate embroideries. If you can't find them in your usual fabric shop, try shops that sell curtain fabrics. Artists' unprimed cotton canvas, available from most art shops, can also be used. The preparation of fabrics for painting is dealt with in Chapter 8.

Organza is an excellent fabric for light-weight embroideries. Because it is semi-transparent, different layers can be embroidered (and also painted) in a coordinated design, then placed one over the other to create a feeling of mood or distance. Unusual effects can be obtained by using various combinations of the wide range of colours available.

Organza is available in both silk and polyester. Silk organza will take the strain of more embroidery than the polyester variety, while polyester is more transparent, and lends itself to the creation of moods. It is generally advisable not to press polyester. If necessary, test a piece with a cool iron before you begin to embroider.

Organza is very adaptable and can be incorporated into many techniques—for instance, appliqué, stumpwork and fabric sculpting. In addition to the layering technique already mentioned, it can be used to soften the coarseness of canvas and calico backgrounds. All these applications are discussed in more detail later.

Pure silk is another fabric suitable for free-machine embroidery, being both firm and closely woven. As the fibres are very fine, however, it is preferable to use it only for light-weight embroideries. Pure silk can be quilted with embroidery, using a thin wadding backed with another fabric, such as a fine muslin, to hold the quilting. Silk can also be painted, with special paints that are clear and transparent. The colours and the lustre of the silk create a unique background.

Some evenweave fabrics, especially linen, are suitable for the various threadwork techniques. This is a specialised area discussed fully in Chapter 6.

Fabrics suitable for free-machine embroidery

2 UNDERSTANDING THE BASICS

Before you can begin to create that special piece of embroidery, you must have a thorough knowledge of a wide range of stitches and techniques.

It is wise to have an extra hoop to practise on. Even when you are very experienced, it can be used for 'warm-up' exercises and to experiment with different tensions, colour combinations and techniques, before applying them to the actual embroidery. This is important, as mistakes are extremely hard to unpick.

Even when you are quite certain of what you are doing, always run the machine first on the practice hoop to make sure no excess oil will spoil your creation. As a sewing machine used for embroidery works at a far higher rate than when it is used for dressmaking, it requires cleaning and oiling every couple of hours, greatly increasing the risk of oil spots. When you clean the machine, remove all the fluff and oil it *lightly* following the manufacturer's instructions in the handbook.

Framing the Hoop

When setting up a hoop for free-machine embroidery the fabric is placed on the underside of the hoop, that is, the opposite way around to hand embroidery techniques. The back of the fabric should be touching the table. This is illustrated in the photograph on page 84 as well as on the previous page.

It is important that the fabric to be worked on in the hoop is pulled firm, evenly stretched and drum-tight. The best way to achieve this is to place the outer ring of the hoop on your work surface, then place the fabric over it right side up—the inner ring of the hoop should then be pressed into the fabric and the outer ring. Check by the warp and weft that the grain is straight, pull carefully if any adjustment is required, then tighten the screw a little. *The fabric must be drum-tight* (tap it to test the sound). When the fabric tension is correct, tighten the screw with a screwdriver.

Fabric which is loose in the hoop will inevitably become distorted and puckered during the embroidery process. Puckers never press out satisfactorily, and should be avoided at all times. Slack fabric can also cause needles to bend or break, threads to snap, and the frequent occurrence of skipped stitches.

I cannot over-emphasise the importance of correctly hooping the fabric before you begin embroidering, and thus preventing all these problems. After all, it is the very foundation of your embroidery.

The size of the fabric to be worked on should be, at the very minimum, a square approximately 10 cm wider than the diameter of the hoop. That is, for a 20 cm hoop cut a piece of fabric 30 cm square. The fabric can be bigger, of course, or rectangular. In these cases you will need to move the hoop to embroider all the larger area. Bear in mind that you will want to avoid crushing the embroidery with the hoop when it is moved. Preliminary planning of where and how to overlap will be valuable.

While using a larger hoop to avoid overlaps might seem logical, in practice it doesn't work. A larger hoop tends to knock the body of the machine as it is turned while you are embroidering. The maximum comfortable working size for a hoop is approximately 20 cm diameter. If the hoop is much larger than this, another difficulty occurs—keeping the fabric taut while working on it. With a large area of stretched fabric the actual motion of the embroidery in progress can slacken the fabric.

Before You Begin

Before you commence an embroidery run through this list of procedures.

• Two hoops should be used. They don't need to be the same size. The smaller one may be your practice hoop, the larger one for the actual embroidery—or the other way around. The two hoops should be filled with the same fabric, stretched evenly in both hoops until it is drum-tight. Tap to check the sound.

• Your sewing machine must be kept clean, free from fluff, and oiled according to the instructions in your handbook.

• The needle must be sharp, never bent or blunt.

• The machine should be threaded in the usual way, using the correct threads for the stitch. (Check with the chart on page 16.) Adjust the tensions if necessary.

• Lower the feed-dog (or cover it with the special cover-plate). Remove the normal sewing foot and replace it with the free-machine embroidery foot, or the darning foot. (You can work without a foot if you prefer, but please be careful, and keep your fingers on the rim of the hoop.)

• Place the practice hoop under the needle, using the flywheel to position the needle at the place where you want to begin.

• Bring the bobbin thread up through the fabric. Hold this thread together with the thread from the needle. Put the needle back into the fabric and *lower the presser foot lever.* This is the most easily forgotten thing, and it is the most important to remember. Whether the foot is on or not, the presser foot bar controls the flow of thread through the needle. If it is left up, you will get a tangle of loops under the fabric. This takes quite a while to remove, as the stitches are very hard to unpick. It is best to remember.

• After lowering the presser foot lever, begin with a few free-running stitches on the spot to secure the threads. Trim the 'tails' after a few more stitches.

• Doodle around to practise. Try out the stitch that you will be using, adjusting the tensions and width if necessary. When you are satisfied with the results secure the threads with on-the-spot free-running, and trim them close to the fabric.

You are now ready to start on the actual embroidery, but always remember the *basic routine.*

BASIC ROUTINE

1 Draw the bobbin thread up through the fabric.

2 Hold the threads from the needle and bobbin together.

3 Position the needle in the fabric at the spot where you want to begin, using the flywheel.

4 *Lower the presser foot lever*—very important.

5 Secure the threads with a few free-running stitches.

6 Begin the embroidery, stopping after a few stitches to trim off the threads.

Twelve Points to Remember

ALWAYS:

1 Work a practice hoop first.

2 Ensure the fabric in the hoop is as tight as a drum.

3 *Lower the presser foot lever* before commencing your work.

4 Start the work with the needle in the fabric.

5 Begin and end with a few small stitches to enable close trimming of the threads.

6 When moving from one part of the work to another, lift the presser foot lever to release the thread, place the needle into the fabric in its new position, then *lower the presser foot lever and start again* with a few small stitches.

7 Move the hoop smoothly—jerky movements break threads and needles.

8 The length of the stitch is determined by you, and depends on the speed of the machine and the movements of the hoop.

9 Keep a chart for experiments, making notes of the stitches used and how they were done—tensions, speed of the machine, speed of the hoop, threads used, etc.

10 Make sure the needle is sharp, not bent or blunt.

11 Keep the machine cleaned and oiled, preferably after every couple of hours work.

12 *Keep experimenting*—try different threads and fabrics and keep notes and examples in your reference book to further your own knowledge. With practice and experimentation there are no limits to what you can do!

3 THE STITCHES AND CHART

Summary Chart of the Stitches

| Stitch | Tension | | Stitch | |
	Top	Bobbin	Length	Width
Free-running	Normal to slightly loose	Normal*	0	0
Free zig-zag and satin fill-in	Slightly loose	Normal to slightly tight	0	Zig-zag 1 to max
Whip stitch	Tighter than normal	Looser than normal	0	0
Feather stitch	Slightly tighter than whip stitch	Slightly looser than whip stitch	0	0
Whip stitch and feather stitch for particular effects	Slightly tighter than normal	Looser than normal— adjust appropriately	0	Zig-zag 1–2

* Normal refers to the normal techniques as used in dressmaking
** Always move the hoop smoothly

This chart, summarising the stitches used in free-machine embroidery, has been found to be very helpful by my students. The chart enables you to tell at a glance the name of a stitch, and all that you need to do to achieve it. Each embroidery stitch has particular requirements—certain threads to be used, tensions adjusted both at the top and in the bobbin.

Because you are working with the feed-dog lowered (or covered with the cover-plate), the length of the stitches is under your control. You determine the length of the stitches by how slowly or quickly you move your work in the hoop. The direction in which you move is also under your control.

The speed of the machine also has an influence on the effects that you seek—if you move your work slowly with the machine running quickly you will soon build up some very nice textures. Conversely, if your machine speed is normal and you move your hoop quickly, you will have long stitches. ('Normal' as I use it here refers to the 'normal' speeds and techniques used in dressmaking.)

Achieving the correct balance between the speed of the machine and the movement of the hoop comes with practice. With the aid of the chart, and

Threads		Speed		Application
Top	*Bobbin*	*Machine*	*Hoop***	
Rayon Cotton Polycotton Polyester	Rayon Cotton Polycotton Polyester	Normal to fast. Steady pace	Try out different movements steadily. Do not jerk	Cornelli & variations Small writing & initials Faces; hair Grasses, bushes & branches Flowers; leaves
Rayon Cotton (fine, #50)	Cotton Polycotton Polyester	Normal to fast	As above. Turn hoop for effect	Writing and initials Trees and bushes Flowers and leaves Feathers, fur Sea, waterfalls
Cotton Polycotton Polyester	Cotton (fine, #50) Rayon	Fast gives more thread on top	Slow— allows the threads to build up	Small writing & initials Directional stitches Bushes & branches Details
Cotton Polycotton Polyester	Cotton (fine, #50) Rayon	Normal to fast	Use small circular movements for a full effect	Cornelli Decorative applications Flower gardens Rocks Wattle flowers
Cotton Polycotton Polyester	Cotton (fine, #50) Rayon	Normal	Slow to medium. Turn hoop for other effects	Useful for building up textures

practising one type of stitch at a time, you will soon get the feeling for it. The various stitches are explained individually and in detail on the following pages. The chart lists all this information for you as well as various applications.

As you become more experienced you will want to try stitches and combinations of your own. Keep notes of these experiments in a chart of your own so that your techniques can improve all the time. A blank chart for this purpose appears at the back of the book (page 108).

The type of thread used is listed on the chart rather than specifying brand names. Suggested brands include, for cottons, DMC 30 and DMC 50, Gütermann 50, Mettler, Molnlycke, Sylko, etc.; for polycotton and polyester, Dewhurst, Duet, Gütermann, Rasant, etc.; for rayon, Isafil, Madeira, Sulky, etc.

Free-running Stitch

Free-running, the first stitch to learn, is a very useful stitch. All the other embroidery stitches begin and end with securing stitches of free-running. Each time you change the colour of the thread, or go from one spot to another, these securing stitches are used. They enable you to trim the threads close to the work without having to pull them through and tie them off with knots.

Not only does free-running have this utility role, it can be as plain or as decorative as you make it. Free-running is good for writing, signing your name on your works, outlines, details, filling-in areas—in almost everything you do, free-running plays an important role.

Machine tensions for free-running are fairly close to normal ('normal' referring to plain dressmaking techniques). Top thread tension can be a fraction looser than normal if necessary, while bobbin tension is normal. Looking at the chart, you can tell at a glance that the stitch length is zero, and the width is zero.

Most threads are compatible with free-running stitch—cottons, rayons, polycottons and metallics. It is usual to work with the same thickness of thread on the top as in the bobbin. Metallic threads are an exception, as a cotton or polycotton can be used in the bobbin instead of another metallic. A Metalfil needle should be used, the larger eye prevents the thread from fraying. Use with a loosened upper tension.

Machine speed for free-running should be normal to fast. Hoop movements should always be smooth. Jerky movements can cause the needle to bend or break and can also cut the threads. So keep calm and work smoothly.

Before you start, check the Basic Routine on page 15. There always seems so much to remember when you first start—like driving a car. It becomes much easier with practice and experience. With the fabric drum-tight in your hoop (preferably calico for practice), the same thread in your machine top and bobbin (cotton thread for now), you are ready to start!

Holding the two threads, with needle in position

A 'doodling' exercise in free-running stitch

Doodles, cornelli and writing in free-running stitch. Halfway down on the right the needle has been removed from one spot to start in another, the thread being left uncut

Free-running on quilted rayon fabric, using a metallic thread on top with loosened tension, cotton below with normal tension

Fireworks

and the presser foot lever down (whether you are using a free-embroidery or darning foot, or the bare needle), commence with the first few stitches to secure the threads. Start to doodle, make squiggles, draw a flower, write your name, whatever takes your fancy—such as on the picture on page 18.

If you want to stop stitching and begin somewhere else, just secure the threads where you stop. Lift the presser foot lever (this releases the tension of the top thread) and move the hooped work to the new position. Reposition the needle using the flywheel,

lower the presser foot lever and, starting with another set of securing stitches, start to embroider again. Snip the thread ends off after a few more stitches—you don't want to embroider them into the work.

When you look closely at the second example, at the top of page 19, which shows some doodles, cornelli and writing, about halfway down on the right you can see where I've gone from one spot to another, with the thread left uncut.

The third example (page 19, bottom) is worked on a rayon fabric, which was padded with thin

Room With a View (oval 21 × 25 cm)

wadding and backed with muslin to make it suitable for quilting. I used a metallic thread on top, and changed the needle to a Metalfil needle. The top tension was loosened. In the bobbin I used cotton thread with a normal tension. On this piece there are just a few squiggles and cornelli, with variations; it shows how free-running can be used to advantage with quilting.

The other example of free-running I have included here portrays exploding fireworks. The fireworks have all been embroidered with free-running—some are done with metallic threads, the others with rayon.

Take a look at the embroidery I have titled *With Apologies to Vincent*, on page 31. You will see how the face, and the beard in particular, are almost entirely embroidered with free-running. I used Isafil, a lovely rayon thread, for the whole picture, as I wanted to pick up light and shade with the shiny threads, in conjunction with the directions of the stitches. *Room With a View* (page 21), is a less elaborate, 'fun' picture done to remind me of a stopover in Europe. It is almost all embroidered in free-running, with some zig-zag and whip stitch, on hand-painted silk.

Free Zig-zag Stitch

Free zig-zag stitch is probably used more widely than any other single stitch in free-machine embroidery. It is most adaptable, being used also in conjunction with such techniques as applied threads, drawn thread work, pulled thread work and wrapping. It is also used to create textures (see Chapter 4, Textures and Directions). Satin fill-in, an extension of free zig-zag, is explained next. I have frequently adapted free zig-zag, and used it together with other stitches, to create special effects. Free zig-zag is so versatile it features in almost every section of this book, especially in Chapter 7, Overlays and Underlays, and Chapter 10, Fabric Sculpting.

Nearly all types of threads can be used in free zig-

This example demonstrates how the free zig-zag stitch worked with the hoop moving slowly gives a satin stitch, and worked with the hoop moving quickly gives an open zig-zag

Zig-zag exercises

zag. The finest results are obtained by using a lighter weight thread on the top, such as a fine cotton (#50) or a rayon, with a thicker thread, an ordinary weight cotton or polycotton, on the bobbin.

The combination of fine rayon on top with a thicker thread below is also especially useful for satin fill-in when colours are being bled into each other. Rayon threads blend together beautifully and pick up light and shade to advantage.

To begin free zig-zag, thread the machine with rayon or fine cotton thread on top, with a matching polycotton or polyester thread on the bobbin. Top tension can range from normal to slightly loose. The bobbin tension is normal to firm.

A heavy duty calico or a firm, closely woven cotton fabric in your practice hoop would be ideal. If you haven't any on hand, regular calico or cotton can be used. They will probably have to be reinforced with an iron-on interfacing. This is necessary because both free zig-zag and satin fill-in tend to 'pull in' the fabric.

You are not generally advised to back fabrics for free-machine embroidery but, because one cannot always obtain a firm, closely woven, pure cotton in attractive colours, it often becomes necessary to compromise. Reinforcement with a good quality interfacing works well. I have used it for most of the examples in this book with good results.

When working free zig-zag you must be very particular about stretching the fabric in your hoop both evenly and drum-tight. Test the sound, and tighten the screw with a screwdriver to make sure the fabric doesn't slip. (The bound inner ring of the hoop also works to control any slackening.)

With fabric stretched and machine threaded, start with the Basic Routine. When you have secured the threads, and before you position the needle, turn the width selector to a medium width. Position the needle now (presser foot lever down) and start to free zig-zag. Use medium machine speed and move the hoop smoothly and positively. You will see from the illustration on page 22 that moving the hoop slowly gives a satin stitch. Moving the hoop quickly gives an open zig-zag. Try this for yourself, remembering that you control the length. This applies to all free-machine embroidery stitches.

Follow the exercises in the picture on page 23. Alter the widths of the zig-zag stitch, try different angles, turn the hoop around. Embroider your initials. Try everything and more!

By using a different colour on the top to the one in the bobbin, and providing that the threads are of the same type and thickness, you can bring up the bobbin thread to just appear at each end of the zig-zag stitch. This is achieved by tightening the top tension just enough to bring up the lower thread. This technique is especially useful for obtaining natural effects, such as leaves or grasses, using two shades of green, for instance. It works best on a small to medium width zig-zag. A large width drags the fabric in too much at this tension.

Free zig-zag can be used for branches, tree trunks, leaves and grasses. It is especially effective using the same weight of thread on top and in the bobbin in different shades of the same colour. Working in this way it is possible to tighten the top tension enough to show the bobbin colour at either end of the stitch, then to drop back to normal. Be prepared to use many shades and combinations of colours to create a natural look.

Satin Fill-in Stitch

Satin fill-in may be compared with the long-and-short stitch of hand embroidery. It works very well using the thinner and finer cotton threads on top, such as DMC 50 or Gütermann's 50 cotton thread, or the

rayon threads such as Isafil, Madeira or Sulky. In the bobbin use a cotton thread for preference, or one of the polycottons. The top tension should be slightly loose, the bobbin tension normal.

The stitching works into itself, the stitches blending or bleeding into each other in overlapping rows. The rows need not be worked in a straight line—in fact, satin fill-in blends more successfully if a slight curve is used.

An overall direction is advisable. For instance, with flower petals the stitches should radiate from the centre and 'drop' at the edges, so that the embroidery

The satin fill-in stitch used in a flower petal should radiate from the centre and drop at the edges

is going in a curved direction one way and at the same time away from the centre. The pansy illustrates this technique.

Various colour combinations can be used to enhance the directional effect, as well as to give light and shade. Remember that the very direction of the stitches will give light and shade also.

Free-running stitches or whip stitch can be used to detail leaf-veins and other markings, perhaps for outlines and shadows.

Satin fill-in can be used for a stem-stitch effect (as with hand embroidery) if guided to make a single line.

Look at the example of a leaf. One half is only partially embroidered to show the directions of the satin fill-in. The stitches become closer so that they overlap at the tip of the leaf. The other side has been completed. The leaf has been outlined using a single line of zig-zag. A rayon thread was used on the top with a slightly loosened tension, a matching coloured cotton thread on the bobbin. Try working some leaves like this for practice.

Satin fill-in and free zig-zag stitches can also be used in a more open way, leaving some of the background fabric showing to give the illusion of depth. This technique is suitable for clouds, sunsets or the sea on appropriately coloured background fabrics—perhaps on a painted background. If you prefer not to paint, similar effects can be embroidered onto a plain coloured fabric, which can be applied to the background later.

Satin fill-in can be used together with free zig-zag for fur, feathers, faces, hair, clothes, to mention just a few. Turn your work to obtain maximum benefit from the direction that these subjects grow in, and to pick up the effects of light and shade.

With Apologies to Vincent, on page 31, demonstrates the satin fill-in technique in the background and on his hat, while free-running was used for his face and beard.

For a coarser, more rugged effect, suitable for trees, leaves, bushes, grasses and so on, satin fill-in using a cotton, polycotton or polyester thread both in the top and in the bobbin is very satisfactory.

Half this leaf has been completed in satin fill-in, the other half left only partly embroidered to show the direction of the stitches

Scorched Trees I (24 cm diameter)
This picture is embroidered entirely with polyester threads. The embroidery demonstrates the variety of textures that can be obtained with free zig-zag and satin fill-in stitches, combined with a few touches of whip stitch and free-running. The background is handpainted heavy-duty calico

Cotton, polycotton and polyester threads come in an extremely good colour range, they are readily available and reasonably priced. I used them exclusively on the *Scorched Trees* pictures (pages 26 and 56), on *Twin Trees At Leura* (page 63), *A Quiet Place* (page 39) and for *Here I Am* (page 65). All these pictures are composed mainly of free zig-zag and satin fill-in stitches. Other stitches include whip stitch and free-running.

Both satin fill-in and free zig-zag stitches can be

used over thick cotton or linen threads to achieve a three-dimensional effect, as described in the Applied Threads and Wrapped Threads sections of Chapter 6.

Whip Stitch

Whip stitch is very much like free-running, the main difference being the richness of colour created by the bobbin thread being brought up to the right side of the fabric by tension adjustments. This forms a raised stitch and becomes the main colour.

For whip stitch, tension adjustments are made by tightening the tension of the top thread (which is of cotton or polycotton and stronger than the lower thread) and loosening the bobbin tension. Use either a fine cotton thread or one of the silky rayon threads in the bobbin.

Loosen the bobbin tension by adjusting the screw on the bobbin case. If your bobbin case is of the fixed type, follow the instructions for loosening tension in the sewing machine's handbook.

If the bobbin case is removeable, as it is in my machine, remove it, and place a filled bobbin in the case and test the normal tension by holding the thread in your fingers and letting the case dangle. It should

Whip stitch exercises

hold its position for normal tension, or maybe drop a little with a flip of the holding hand.

Fractional adjustments of the tiny screw on the side of the bobbin case will alter the tension. (Do this cautiously. The screw is very tiny—it can fly out and disappear for a long time!) The altered tension for whip stitch should allow the threaded bobbin case to slide slowly down the thread under its own weight.

If you are serious about free-machine embroidery, I really do recommend that you buy a second bobbin case especially for whip stitch and feather stitch where the bobbin tension is always loosened. You will also have the convenience of your normal bobbin case set and ready for use at all times.

Thread the machine, using a cotton or polycotton thread on top of a different colour to that of the rayon or fine cotton thread in the bobbin. This way you can really see what happens. If you look closely at the photograph on page 27, you will realise that I have used the background colour, purple, on the top and a shade of pink for the rayon thread in the bobbin. All you can see at first glance is the pinky colour. Only when I spread out the stitch with a quicker movement of the hoop does the upper thread appear—on the left side of the photograph.

Follow the Basic Routine carefully after filling your practice hoop with calico or similar. Try out a few stitches and then doodle. Is the lower thread coming up as it should? If not, tighten the top tension very

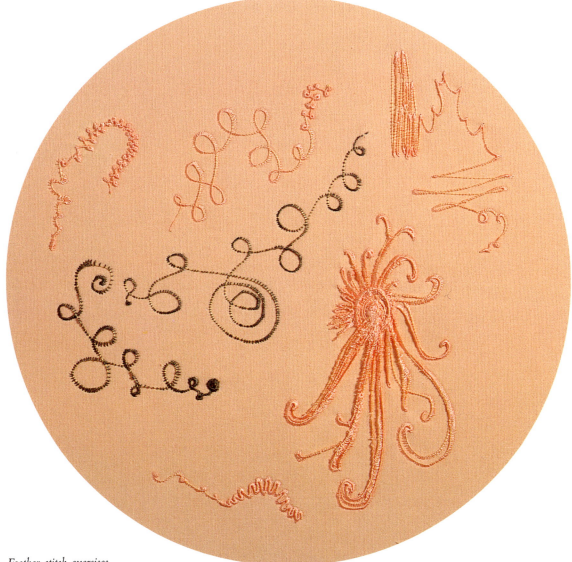

Feather stitch exercises

slightly more. If the thread breaks in use, it is too tight—loosen it to where it was. The lower tension will then need to be adjusted. Loosen the bobbin case screw again very slightly. Try the dangle test.

Start again, remembering to do the Basic Routine. Work your machine fairly quickly now. Move the hoop slowly, allowing the threads to build up. Small writing, bushes and branches, outlines, doodles, squiggles and flower shapes are all good practising material. Keep practising and experimenting!

The 'lace' on the sand in *Sea Lace* (page 37) is almost entirely embroidered with whip stitch. The picture *Underwater Garden* (page 69) is nearly all whip stitch, worked on layers of organza. Feather stitch, the next stitch we will do, has been used here too.

Whip stitch can be used to create rich textures and combines well with feather stitch. It is discussed in detail in Chapter 4, Textures and Directions, and Chapter 7, Overlays and Underlays.

Feather Stitch

Feather stitch really has the feathery look its name implies. Some embroiderers refer to it as 'exaggerated whip stitch', which is also quite accurate, as you will see from the way it is achieved. The threads used are also the same as for whip stitch—that is, cotton or polycotton through the top and rayon or a fine cotton in the bobbin.

The tensions are then exaggerated—the top is very slightly tighter than whip stitch, but not so tight that it breaks. The bobbin tension can be so loose that when you do the dangle test the weight of the bobbin in its case must be supported with the other hand. Be careful that you don't make it so loose that

the holding screw jumps out. As a double check, hold the bobbin in its case with one hand and draw the thread up with the other. The thread should run out smoothly. (For whip stitch, the thread in this test would have a slightly controlled run-out.)

On a fixed bobbin case, all you need to do is turn the special screw a bit more, maybe even as far as it will go.

When you have made these adjustments, thread the machine with a different coloured polycotton or polyester thread on the top to that of the rayon or fine cotton you have in the bobbin.

Use calico or a similar cotton fabric in the practice hoop. Follow the Basic Routine instructions and start off with circles and loops. Move the hoop slowly, but work the machine at a normal to fast speed. If the lower thread is not coming up in loops, just go through the tension adjustments again, increasing the top tension first (but not to breaking point). If that is not enough, loosen the bobbin tension as before, taking great care not to lose that all-important screw. It needs to be there, and to stay there when your machine is in action.

Have a look at the example on the opposite page, where you will see some of the round shapes, squiggles, circles and loops that feather stitch is so good for. It makes beautiful textures, too. Do some yourself, allowing the lower thread to come up in loops and then fall into shape.

I used this stitch on the 'wings' at the top of the picture *Impressions of Jenolan Caves* (page 91), which is described on page 104 in the Fabric Sculpting chapter. The froth and foam in *Sea Lace* (page 37) was done in feather stitch, embroidered first on butter muslin and then applied, a technique described in Chapter 4, Textures and Directions.

Feather stitch works well with whip stitch. They are seen together in *Underwater Garden* (page 69) and in Chapter 7, Overlays and Underlays.

4 TEXTURES AND DIRECTIONS

The directions of embroidered stitches can create perspective, roundness and movement, giving shape and meaning to your subject. The stitches themselves pick up light and shade, acting rather like the pencil strokes in a sketch. The use of carefully chosen colours can bring reality closer, something like a painting.

Vincent van Gogh's paintings are full of strongly directional brushwork. In copying one of his self-portraits as an exercise I learned a lot—his unusual combinations of colours, together with his strong brush strokes, give great texture and direction to the paint.

My first step was to paint his picture onto heavy-duty calico using fabric paints. Then I completely covered the fabric with free-running, satin fill-in, free zig-zag and whip stitch. In the photograph you can see how the directions of the stitches pick up plenty of light and shade. I used a rayon thread on the top with a normal to slightly released tension for most of the work, in the bobbin using a cotton thread with a normal to firm tension. The exception to this was the whip stitch on parts of his beard, where the threads and tensions are reversed.

With Apologies to Vincent (oval 17 × 20 cm)

Appliqué

This picture of six circles shows how appliqué comes to life with the use of directional stitches. Six circles of coloured fabric have been bonded onto the background, but only three have been embroidered. Using free-running stitches, the directions of the embroidery make the circles appear more rounded than the plain circles. This is an exercise worth doing.

Still Life below shows appliqué bonded to the background fabric. The directions of the free-running and free zig-zag stitches with the careful choice of colour imply roundness, texture, shininess and shadow. This gives dimension to the otherwise flat appliquéd pieces. Do make something similar for yourself.

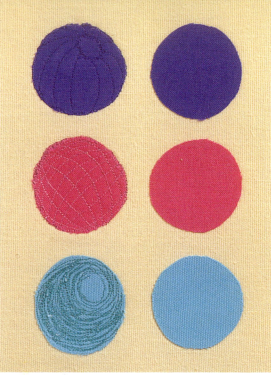

Appliqué circles

Still Life
Appliqué given added dimension by the careful choice of colours and directional stitches

Quilting

Quilting also creates dimension and textures. The free-running exercise on page 19 is done on a padded rayon fabric. The example on page 81 demonstrates free-running with free zig-zag and openwork techniques on a painted silk background, with thin wadding and muslin behind the work for quilting purposes. Both these pieces have been embroidered with metallic threads using a Metalfil needle.

Water

Interesting ocean and still water effects can be created using free zig-zag stitch on an appropriate shade of blue-green fabric or, better still, on a hand-painted sea, river or lake. In the example below I have demonstrated the basic directions you can take with just four blue-green shades—first separately, and then intermingling them.

Try this on your practice hoop, using as many harmonising colours as you have. By changing the direction of the stitches you can make waves or suggest a swell on the ocean. I have deliberately left the background fabric just showing in various places to give further movement and depth.

When you are embroidering a sea picture, the sea at the horizon can be commenced with free-running, moving to a tiny zig-zag (maybe in a more subdued colour, depending on the light of the sky). The stitches become wider as you move forward from the horizon, revealing more detail in the directions of the waves. Colour variations add to the effect.

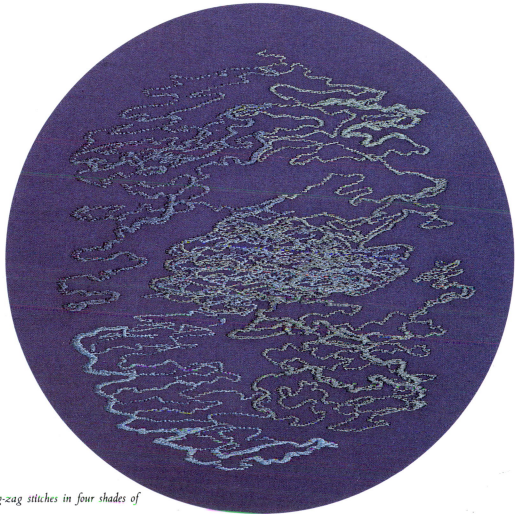

Sea exercise using free zig-zag stitches in four shades of blue-green

Textures

Wonderful textures can be created using just free zig-zag, whip stitch and feather stitch. Experiment on the practice hoop, but generally you will find it best to work the machine quickly, and move the hoop slowly for this work. Use miniature cornelli patterns and tiny circular movements to allow the threads to build up and form the desired textures.

Lines up, down and around and close together give another type of texture and will pick up light and shade. This will enhance the directions of your stitches even when only one colour has been used. The photograph shows the different movements that can be created by whip stitch and feather stitch.

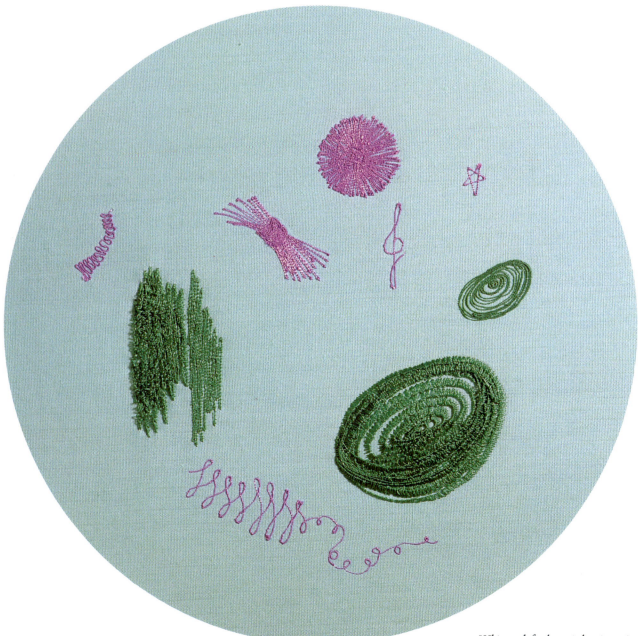

Whip and feather stitches in action

Butter Muslin (gauze)

For a richer texture, butter muslin (gauze) can be used, embroidered separately from the picture, then cut out and appliquéd. The butter muslin is stretched into the hoop in the usual way (below), making sure that the weave is straight in both directions. Starting with a few small running stitches to secure the threads, use a zig-zag stitch to pull the loosely woven threads of the butter muslin together—it is really quite fascinating watching this happen. You can experiment with stitch widths, turning the hoop, working up, down and crossways and in a small circular motion. Look at the picture on page 36. Working diagonally across the butter muslin gives a rounder result. Holes can be poked into the butter muslin with a knitting needle and worked around, or over and across, using openwork techniques.

Try using a rayon thread in the bobbin with a looser than normal tension. Use a cotton or poly-cotton thread on top of another colour. The top tension should be tighter than normal (the usual set-up for whip stitch and feather stitch), but in this case, use a small to medium width zig-zag. This pulls in the butter muslin and gives a very rich whip stitch or feather stitch, depending on how much you have adjusted the tensions. Experiment! Use slow, tiny,

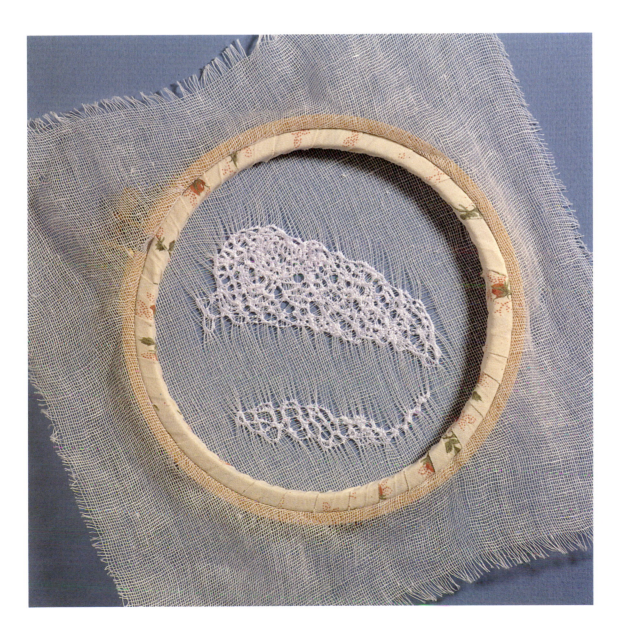

Exercises on butter muslin using different threads and stitches

circular movements and work your machine medium to fast. I am sure that you will be delighted with the results. Try different colour combinations too.

For floral gardens, try painting the butter muslin with fabric paints before you start. Have bobbins filled with as many colours as you want to use—it is easy enough to change the bobbin. You could use a leaf colour in a cotton thread on the top. After the worked butter muslin has been applied to the main fabric, other leaf colours can be added and extended. Use details such as tall flowers and shrubs, and extra colours, to blend the piece into the picture.

The surf in the picture *Sea Lace* was created in a similar way. Using rayon threads, in many shades of white through to a pale aqua, I filled a number of bobbins first. On the top I used a near-white cotton thread, and a slightly tight tension. The loosened bobbin case was in use, releasing the flow of thread to produce texture. Small holes were encouraged in the butter muslin to give depth and reveal the painted colours of the sea beneath the foam. The surf in the distance was embroidered directly onto the picture itself with proportionally smaller stitches. The embroidered butter muslin was cut and

Sea Lace (24 × 25 cm)

fitted to the nearer parts of the picture. The edges of the appliqué were disguised by embroidering froth and foam over and around with plenty of movement and feeling.

This technique brings an added dimension to a picture. By bringing the front forward it pushes the back of the picture further away, thereby creating depth and distance.

Another advantage of using butter muslin for this kind of work is a very practical one. With so much heavy embroidery the background fabric could become distorted. The butter muslin takes the strain of all this independently, thus giving a rich texture without overworking the background fabric.

Leaves and Grasses

Leaves and grasses can be created by using free-running stitches together with free zig-zag. When using free zig-zag you need to turn your work sideways or at an angle to get the natural look of grasses growing, or of certain leaves that mainly hang downwards or at a slight angle, such as gum leaves. Vary the widths of the stitch, and the shades of green.

I always embroider with at least three shades of a colour, using a different one in the bobbin from the one on the top. This way, I can alter the top tension to bring up the bobbin colour, and therefore use the two colours simultaneously. It's best to use the same type of threads top and bobbin when doing this kind of work. Study the tree and leaf exercise below. *Scorched Trees I* and *II* on pages 26 and 56 also demonstrate this technique.

To embroider long grasses, work the distant ones

Tree and leaf exercises

A Quiet Place (25 cm diameter)

first using free-running stitches. Work in imaginary layers, moving forward, becoming larger, clearer and more defined as the layers get closer to the front of the picture. The grasses can be made to grow in a particular direction, or to look windswept. Using a fawn colour in the bobbin, grass seeds will appear as you run back and forth. Shorter, tufty grasses in free zig-zag look natural—turn the work sideways for this. Details can be added with free-running or whip stitch, as can bushes and front row trees—work trunks and branches first, adding the leaves over them. *A Quiet Place* demonstrates the use of all these techniques.

5 OPENWORK

Openwork with free-machine embroidery compares with machine darning. Perhaps it evolved from this humble beginning!

Openwork can be used to enhance clothing, household items, wall hangings and pictures. Coloured backdrops add to the elegance of the embroidery.

Openwork is very compatible with drawn thread work, which is basically vertical or horizontal. Openwork can be spun across in any direction and so extends the limits of drawn thread work, adding to its uses. All the pictures in Chapter 6, Fabric Threads, incorporate openwork techniques.

Method

Openwork begins with small holes being cut from the fabric, but only after their perimeters have been reinforced. Webs of free-running are spun across the open area, decorating and connecting with lines and lace. Spider's webs can be formed. Lines can be crossed geometrically, or in an abstract way. Larger designs and patterns may require a strengthened, thicker webbing, achieved by spinning a second line of webbing on or next to the first line. With a small to medium zig-zag stitch the two lines are bound together, the result resembling Richelieu embroidery.

Webs, darning and lacy effects can all be used to fill in areas of openwork

Some of the many ways of using the spider's web technique

The most satisfying results are achieved on a fine, firm, closely woven cotton or linen. If you find in practice that your chosen fabric is not quite firm enough, try strengthening it with some iron-on interfacing. For practising, calico is quite suitable, and it too can be interfaced if necessary.

Rayon or cotton threads are good for openwork. It is important to use the same thickness of thread on top and in the bobbin to maintain an even balance. The threads should twist over each other equally to form a web.

Start with a normal tension on the top and the bobbin tension normal to firm. You will need to use the free-embroidery foot or the darning foot.

To begin with, an all-cotton thread is preferable. Use the same colour as the fabric and thread your

Various designs using openwork. Two bars have been covered with free satin stitch

machine with it, top and bobbin. (The examples have been embroidered in black and coloured threads to make the technique visible.)

On your practice fabric finely mark out three shapes to practise on—circles are good for first attempts. A small triangle or square is also suitable—perhaps one of each. The shapes can be marked out from paper templates. If you have a geometrical template use it to draw the shapes you want on the paper. When you have cut them out, arrange them on the fabric and mark around them finely and accurately with a well sharpened hard pencil or a tailor's chalk pencil. You don't want these lines to show through the embroidery.

Stretch the fabric evenly and firmly in the hoop, drum-tight. Tap to test the sound as usual. Place the

Shisha can be used in openwork to great effect. Tree and fish skeletons lend themselves readily to openwork

hoop under the needle, positioning the needle into one of the outlines on the fabric. Presser foot lever down! Draw up the bobbin thread and hold the two threads. Secure the threads before following the outline around two or three times, keeping the lines of stitching close together. These stitch lines help to strengthen the fabric structure. Repeat this procedure with the second and third shapes. End off and trim the threads. The picture on page 40 shows this step by step.

Turn the hoop so that the underside of the fabric is to the top. With small, finely pointed scissors cut a tiny slit in the centre of the first shape, then cut to the inside of the outline stitching. Cut as neatly and closely as you can without cutting into the supporting stitches. Cut out the other two shapes in the same way. If you prefer, the pieces can be cut with the fabric out of the hoop.

If you want to work with a different coloured cotton thread, change it now. Reposition the hooped fabric under the needle. Check the Basic Routine, then go around the outline once or twice with free-running. This gives you a good strong base to work from.

Openwork can create the effect of a rock painting

You are now ready to make a web. Relax and think of the direction of the web before you start—remember, jerky movements will snap the threads and maybe the needle as well.

Darning or weaving can be used as a decorative fill-in. Web your way to the opposite side of the open space. Secure the thread there and come back. Keep going back and forth until the space is filled in. Turn your work 90° and cross over the newly spun threads, going back and forth as before. If the weave is not close enough for you, go over it again. On the demonstration circle I doubled up on a small section of the darning to show the difference (page 41).

Lacy effects can be created by running a web across one side or corner of the open shape, as I did in the square. Using a free-running stitch (or a tiny zig-zag) work in small circular movements, catching the web and then the outline of the shape. Only do a small section at a time. Keep adding a web and filling it in with 'lace' circles. You may want to stop at a lacy border or to go all the way, filling the entire area. It is quite fascinating to create lace in space.

Now for a spider's web. These are shown in the purple and yellow triangle on page 41, and also on page 42. Web your way to the other side of the open space,

with your machine running evenly and yourself confident. When you get to the opposite side, secure the threads there, and run to the next spot. Come back to the other side at another angle, crossing the first web in the centre or nearby. Do this again so there are three (or four if you like) webs right across the centre. Make a whorl, starting in the middle like a spider's web. Do all this positively and without hesitation.

It is necessary to neaten the outlines after the spaces have been filled and decorated. First, trim the work carefully with small sharp scissors. You could also use a small free zig-zag to tidy away any little wisps of fabric thread too minute to trim. Go around the outline edges with the stitch just close enough to disguise and neaten.

Start now to decorate and finish with a border of free-running, or whip stitch if you prefer. Move in small circles or squiggles, or use lines worked backwards and forwards from the edge, but radiating as though from the centre of the shape. A small to medium free zig-zag can be utilised in any of the above ways. A close medium-width free satin stitch can be embroidered around the edges if you like.

A very neat and formal edge is achieved by using a close machine satin stitch, with or without cording,

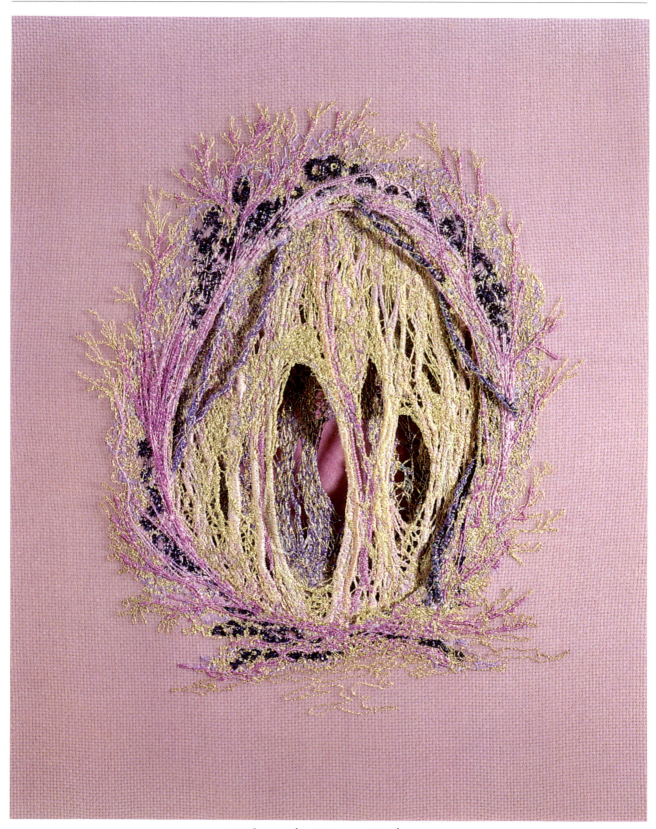

Where the Fairies Hide (22 × 24 cm)

rather in the manner of a machined buttonhole. You will need to use the appropriate foot, and bring the feed-dog up (or remove the cover-plate), for this. Keep the work taut by leaving it in the hoop. The satin stitch should be at right angles to the edge of the openworked area all the way around. Make sure there is sufficient room for the work to be turned without the hoop bumping into the body of the machine. A smaller hoop, 16 to 18 cm in diameter, is often useful in these circumstances.

Metallic threads give good results with openwork. The lacy techniques seem to suit this thread best. Use a Metalfil needle with metallic threads. The eye is larger than that of an ordinary machine needle, and this prevents the thread from fraying as it comes through. The top tension needs to be eased slightly. The bobbin remains at normal. Try it out first, before the actual piece.

More Openwork Exercises

Prepare another practice piece with three open spaces, as before.

1 Try out a double web, binding the threads together with a small to medium zig-zag stitch. Experiment with other webs, using this technique.

2 Use rayon threads on top and in the bobbin. Try webbing in as many patterns as you can think of.

3 Try out metallic threads for another exercise, on top and in the bobbin. Remember to use the Metalfil needle and a slightly loosened tension on the top, with a normal tension on the bobbin. Examples of metallic thread work appear on page 44. Mirror sequins (shisha) can be incorporated into this kind of work.

Problem-solving

Openwork can present a few problems.

• If the thread keeps breaking, even though you have loosened the tensions slightly, try using a tiny zig-zag stitch. It will look just like free-running, but will not break as easily.
• If your machine can do a very wide zig-zag stitch, and so has a stitch plate wider than usual, it will offer less support than other machines for the openwork webbing. In these cases using the darning foot, and the tiny zig-zag, will overcome the problem.
• Always check that the needle is straight and sharp—and that your machine is cleaned and oiled.
• Balanced tensions are most important for openwork. Usually when there is a problem the top tension needs to be slightly loosened. Sometimes the bobbin tension needs to be adjusted. Always alter the tensions very slightly.
• Don't despair if you end up with knots and loops instead of lovely openwork. Just cut them away and start again on the space!

Openwork is a beautiful technique and well worth perfecting. The ability to put threads across space is a useful art in the realms of free-machine embroidery, and can be used in very many ways, as you will see. Persevere, experiment and be creative!

Pictures which incorporate openwork techniques include *Where the Fairies Hide* (page 46), *Impressions of Wombeyan Caves* (page 48), *Trees in the Blue Mountains* (page 54), *A Canopy of Kelp* (page 70), and *Impressions of the Imperial Cave* (page 98). Openwork used together with quilting on painted silk is shown on page 81.

6 FABRIC THREAD TECHNIQUES

Impressions of Wombeyan Caves (20 cm diameter)

Pulled Thread Work

Pulled thread work, using butter muslin (gauze), has already been touched on in Chapter 4 (page 35). You will remember from that exercise how the threads were pulled together with a zig-zag stitch, creating a textured effect. This was using pulled thread work in a constructive way.

In this section we will deal with pulled thread work in a more formal, though decorative, manner. This will mean keeping to the line of the woven thread. A loosely woven fabric of linen or cotton can be used—even some curtain fabrics are suitable.

The two pillars of pulled thread work in the photograph below are different, even though they have been worked identically with the same cotton thread and free zig-zag of the same width. The only difference in their construction was the use of a wing needle (which also appears in the photograph).

The wing needle is designed for threadwork. The wings push the threads of the fabric apart, enlarging the spaces between them. Carefully check the width of the zig-zag stitch before you begin using the wing

Pulled thread work exercises

needle. The wings must clear the free embroidery foot, or darning foot, as well as the edges of the stitch plate.

When you are embroidering more formally, using the in-built machine embroidery stitches, remember to check for the same clearances with whichever foot you are using. Lovely borders can be achieved using these decorative stitches. Withdrawing some of the horizontal threads before you begin can be a great help with such borders, as accuracy is all important. The woven thread and the stitches have to be in harmony. The photograph below illustrates this technique on a small sachet.

In the photograph on the previous page the rest of the exercise was embroidered using a ballpoint needle, to avoid piercing the fabric threads. It was all done with a free zig-zag stitch, not always with the same width. For the sample on the top left, I embroidered the edges of the border first, keeping straight with the woven thread, going very slowly. In the middle, I let the stitches pull in the threads, going up, down and diagonally.

Cotton thread was used through the top and bobbin for the large pointed window. The tension was normal to slightly loose on the top and normal on the bobbin.

The wavy lines are of free zig-zag close together, forming a satin stitch. I used different widths for each wavy line.

Try these or similar exercises yourself. Pulled thread embroideries can be enhanced by using a suitably coloured fabric for an underlay.

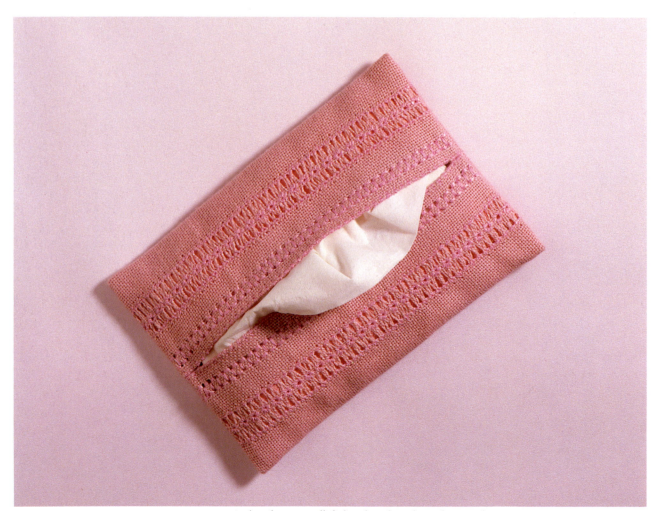

Sachet showing pulled thread work with machine stitches

Drawn Thread Work

Drawn thread work is so called because threads are withdrawn from the fabric. Selected threads are cut and removed, leaving 'exposed' threads in the fabric. Traditionally the exposed threads are grouped together in regular patterns and held with special hand embroidery stitches, including needleweaving, to form decorative patterns and borders.

Drawn thread work can be used to decorate tablecloths, screens, curtains, cushions, hangings and lampshades. Clothing can also be ornamented with decorative borders and panels. Because of its open nature, drawn thread work can be overlaid onto various backgrounds, thus acquiring a different character. Drawn thread work using free-machine embroidery can be very liberated and full of texture, often a far cry from the formality of the hand work from which it is derived.

Loosely woven fabric, mainly with an even weave, is generally used for drawn thread work. Linen, scrim and some furnishing fabrics are suitable. Evenweave linens are especially desirable, ranging all the way from fine to coarse. Linen fibres are strong and lasting. When a lot of work is going into an embroidery it is worthwhile to use a fabric which can withstand the heavy pull of the work as well as endure the test of time.

The threads can be drawn from the fabric in one or both directions of the weave. They can be contained in a shape—freeform or geometrical—or withdrawn in a straight line.

Drawn thread work pictures give your imagination tremendous scope. The work can be overlaid or underlaid with more drawn thread worked on a separate piece. To give depth or mood, it can be backed with other fabrics such as velvet, silk, organza, felt or even leather. Appliqué and embroidery can be incorporated into any of these backdrops. Painted backgrounds are especially useful and give a lot of depth or light to a picture, depending upon the colours used.

Drawn thread work can be greatly enhanced by combining it with pulled thread work and openwork techniques. *Where the Fairies Hide* on page 46 is an example of this combination.

For formal work on clothes or household items, it is most often appropriate to embroider with the same colour, or one to harmonise with the linen background. To create particular effects for pictures or wall hangings use whatever colours work best!

In many examples of drawn thread work it is usual to completely cover the exposed threads of the fabric. Cotton, polycotton and rayon threads are all suitable for the technique. The top thread in the machine can be a different colour and thickness to that in the bobbin. Tensions can be altered to gain a different effect. In the main you will be using a zig-zag stitch. Try cotton threaded through the top of the machine, and a rayon thread in the bobbin with the tension slightly loosened. You will pick up some of the bobbin colour on the outer sides of the linen threads you are covering. Alternatives, experiments and colour combinations should always be tried out first in the practice hoop, which should have the same fabric in it as you will be using for your creation.

When using a loosely woven fabric you need to secure the weave by first of all machining around the outside edges to stop any fraying. I use a wide, open zig-zag or the running stitch on my machine, sewing in the normal way. When you have done this, outline the shape you intend to use before removing any threads. If it is to be a straight block, mark it out with dots using a well sharpened tailor's chalk pencil, carefully following the woven thread lines. If you are only going to pull out threads in one direction, machine sew the two opposite ends of the block, as in the straight-sided shape on page 52. Then cut the threads accurately on the inner sides of the stitching, snipping and removing one thread at a time.

For a geometric or freeform shape, draw it first on a piece of paper. Cut around the outline to make a template. Place this template on the linen and mark around it carefully, using tiny dots of chalk pencil. Machine along the dots to form the outline, using an ordinary straight stitch. If it is a very unusual shape—free forms often are—you may find it easier to put the fabric into the hoop at this point, and free-machine around the outline using free-running stitch. Remove it from the hoop before withdrawing any threads.

The next step is to remove the chosen threads from the linen. This has to be done with care and in good light. Using a thick tapestry needle and a pair of sharply pointed scissors, snip the first thread to be removed. Ease it out gently with the tapestry needle. Once you have followed the thread all the way to the opposite side, cut it off. The first thread is always the hardest to remove. Remove the other threads in a similar way. Keep the threads for future use, unless they are very short. (More about this later.)

If you are removing threads from a large area, it is helpful to leave a couple of horizontal threads

Linen prepared for drawn thread work

approximately halfway down to hold the vertical linen threads in place while you are working. If you haven't left any, and find out later that it would have been useful, don't despair. Simply machine stitch a line or two horizontally across the linen threads. The machine threads can be trimmed away after they have served their purpose (but do this before completing the embroidery, otherwise they can become difficult to remove neatly). The tree embroidery-in-progress on the next page shows the technique.

When you have withdrawn all the required threads, place the piece of linen evenly into the hoop. The linen should be firmly stretched, but with slightly more emphasis on the vertical threads. If you pull too much in the direction of the removed threads, the remaining ones tend to open up. Keep the weave straight in both directions.

Try working the two exercises illustrated in this photograph. For the first one, mark out a small block on an evenweave fabric. Stitch down each end, slit each side carefully, then withdraw the threads. Have the fabric evenly placed and stretched with care in

your practice hoop. Thread the machine with cotton, both top and bobbin. Start with the usual few free-running stitches to secure the threads. Turn the width selector to a medium to wide zig-zag stitch (the length is always zero). Run up and down the exposed fabric threads, allowing them to be drawn together by the stitches. You can run from one group to another to form some kind of pattern. Try a web or two, using the openwork technique (page 42). Then go over it again, producing a satin stitch with the zig-zag to cover any exposed threads of the fabric.

For the second exercise, cut a small circle or freeform shape from paper. Mark around it on the linen with fine dots, using a chalk pencil. Free-machine the outline with free-running. Remove some of the threads from this enclosed area. I would suggest that you remove threads from both directions, leaving some vertical and some horizontal threads to practice on. Start to free zig-zag them together. You will need to turn the work at right angles to catch the horizontal threads. Change the stitch to free-running or a tiny width zig-zag. Now make a web across

Trees in progress, showing the use of a few horizontal threads to hold the tree trunks in place temporarily

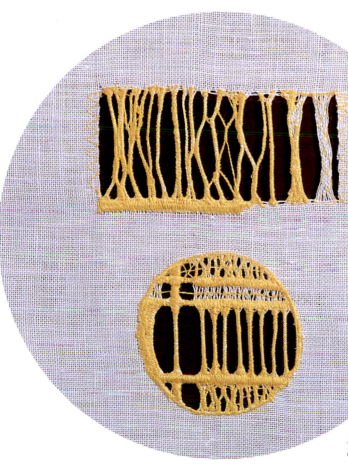

Drawn thread exercises. These are fully described in the text on page 52

Trees in the Blue Mountains (35 × 20 cm)

diagonally, using openwork. Finish off the embroidery using free satin stitch.

Drawn thread techniques can be used for many subjects, in particular those that have a pronounced vertical and/or horizontal character—archways and pillars, buildings, poles and fences, trees, bridges, underwater scenes, rocks, caves and more.

Impressions of Wombeyan Caves, which opens this chapter on page 48, was almost entirely embroidered

using drawn thread techniques, combined with webbing from openwork techniques. *Impressions of the Imperial Cave*, which appears much later on (page 98), was also created in this way, with the addition of fabric sculpting. In both pictures rayon embroidery threads were used throughout.

Trees in the Blue Mountains was embroidered using mainly drawn thread techniques, but incorporating openwork also. The background is layered, using

shadow appliqué and free-machine embroidery. Polyester threads only were used on this picture.

The complex picture *Where the Fairies Hide* (page 46) is partially embroidered with rayon threads. Silver metallic threads festoon the vertical shapes, using openwork webs and lace. Freely embroidered whip stitch, free-running and free zig-zag decorate the irregularly shaped border. The coordinated layer behind is composed of drawn threads held together and embroidered with openwork techniques. Various coloured metallic threads were used with a Metalfil needle. (Looser than normal tensions on the top and in the bobbin were required.) The backdrop fabric is silk. The front overlay is silk organza embroidered with free-running, whip stitch and feather stitch using rayon and metallic threads. Wrapped threads were intertwined before applying them to the picture.

Scorched Trees II (30 × 20 cm)

Applied Threads

The technique of applied threads is very useful, allowing the embroiderer the use of threads that are too thick to go through the needle or the bobbin case. Applied threads compare with the couching of hand embroidery, thick threads being free-machined onto the fabric with either free zig-zag or free-running. These threads can be hand held, or pinned, in the required design or direction, then free-machined. The matching machine thread soon disappears into the thickness of the applied thread.

Many different threads can be used for this

technique. The thicker types of knitting or crochet wools and yarns, both crinkled and plain, embroidery threads, metallics and thin cords, to name but a few, can be used for all kinds of decorative designs and ideas—on cushions, curtains, wallhangings, clothes and so on.

I use applied threads in a constructive manner, for example, as the base for the tree trunk in the foreground of *Scorched Trees II*. The technique is demonstrated in the next photograph. Linen or thick cotton threads are held in place by free-running in a zig-zag direction. The thick threads are covered and built up. Free zig-zag was used initially, building up to satin fill-in which was used both vertically and horizontally. Various coloured threads, both cotton and polyester, were used through the needle, and the bobbin held a cotton thread. The background was heavy duty calico to take the strain of the thick embroidery.

Applied threads work well on wool, linen and cotton, as long as the fabrics are firm, closely woven and thick enough to take the amount of embroidery that you plan to use.

For a practice piece calico is very good. Stretch it carefully and evenly in your hoop. Test for the drum sound. Select the thick threads you intend to apply. The threads must be longer than the design's length because their ends have to disappear into the fabric, a tapestry needle being used to take them through to the back. They are secured underneath with hand stitching.

The next picture shows a few techniques you should try. The first example, a metallic thread, was pinned down. With matching threads top and bobbin, free zig-zag was used to stitch it in place (removing the pins in time to avoid breaking the needle). The ends were neatened by threading them through the fabric and stitching them down by hand.

The straight threads of the orange tapestry wool were first held down with free-running. Free satin stitch was then used over one and then two threads.

The white cotton threads are there to show a corner and how four strands can be held with free-running used in a large zig-zag direction. This is an early exercise of applied threads being used in a constructive way.

The round shape in orange tapestry wool is interesting to do. The outline is finely marked on the fabric—any shape will do, but in this case a circle was used. The wool is held in one hand, the hoop guided with the other. Start on the outline, carefully following it around using free-running with a matching thread in the machine. As you meet the first end of wool make sure you keep it on the inside of the outline. Cover it over as you spiral around, and trim it off on the first or second time around.

The applied threads technique used for the main tree in Scorched Trees II, *showing the thick threads covered and built up with free zig-zag and satin fill-in*

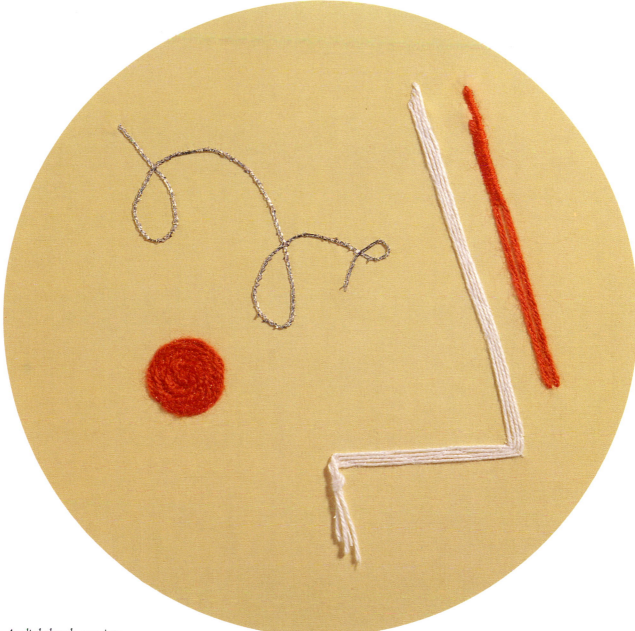

Applied threads exercises

Keep spiralling until you are in the centre. Secure the machine stitches as usual. Thread the remaining wool to the other side of the fabric using the tapestry needle. Secure neatly and trim. Try some other shapes and squiggles with applied threads.

If you are using the applied threads technique for a large piece, you can mark out your design over the fabric and then work your way through it in sections, depending on how much will fit into your hoop.

Applied threads can be worked in another way, using the decorative or utility stitches of your machine in the normal manner (that is, with the appropriate foot on and the feed-dog up). Thick threads can be embellished with decorative stitches, or attached in a more utilitarian way, or even almost invisibly with straight stitching with a matching thread. Practise it first.

Wrapped Threads

The wrapped thread technique provides a use for all those long linen threads withdrawn from your drawn thread pieces. If you haven't any, or want to experiment with other threads, try the thick cotton used for knitting or crochet. Stranded embroidery threads can also be used, especially if you want some of the base colour showing. Knobbly threads partially covered show through in a very decorative way. Using this technique, you can create your own braids and cords for pictures, clothing, decorative hangings and edgings.

The machine can be threaded with the same type of thread top and bobbin, or any of the threads in combination. Colour plays an important part, because the braid or cord can be viewed all around. It can also be deliberately twisted to show off the different colours.

A Canopy of Kelp on page 70 shows many lengths of green stranded cotton combined and almost covered with rayon thread in different greens and blues. The resulting cord was couched partly by hand to the background. Applied thread techniques were also used.

To work this technique you need threads at least 15 cm long for comfortable control. Several

Wrapped threads exercises, with cords (above) wrapped in dense satin fill-in, and flat braids (below) meshed together with zig-zag stitches

thicknesses are required because they squash together once they are bound. The number of threads you use depends on what you want to achieve and how thick or thin the basic threads are.

Group the threads together and hold them firmly, one hand at either end. No hoop is necessary. Your hands will pull the threads to achieve the same result.

To make a cord, hold the bunch of threads under the free embroidery foot (or darning foot) of the sewing machine. Lower the presser foot lever as usual. Holding the threads firmly, begin with a few securing stitches, then turn the stitch width to a wide zig-zag. The first few zig-zag stitches can be worked forwards and backwards for extra security. The loose machine threads can then be trimmed off, or bound in with the thick ones. Cover the thick threads with free zig-zag, going back and forth until a rich satin stitch is achieved. A variety of colours can be incorporated, but in this case leave some areas on the cord only thinly covered, so that when you go over with other colours or metallic thread the cord does not become too thick or hard.

Braids can be made by starting in another way. Instead of free zig-zag, use a free-running stitch in a zig-zag direction to bind the threads together. This keeps the base threads flat. The picture opposite shows cords and braids at different stages. The braid can be kept flat by using a medium width zig-zag and working along the sides and down the middle, meshing the stitches together, as in satin fill-in.

Try working these examples. They are a helpful exercise before moving on to the next development of the wrapping technique, tree skeletons.

Tree Skeletons

Using wrapped threads is a wonderful way to create a tree, especially if you are hesitant to draw one (and even when you are not). It helps to study sketches, photographs or pictures of the type of tree you want to embroider. Have them around you for reference. Think trees!

With strands of threads you can form a tree skeleton. Threads of linen, crochet or knitting cotton, and stranded embroidery threads are all suitable. The threads should be slightly longer than the tree. When they are pulled into the trunk, and their branches spread out, some of their height is lost. The amount of thread required depends on the thickness of the trunk, though if you underestimate more can be added quite easily.

Use the braid technique described on the previous page. Hold the threads very firmly as you join the threads of the trunk, using a free-running stitch in zig-zag directions. The two photographs on the next page show the steps progressively. Spread out the thick threads where the branches are to be.

Use free zig-zag, developing it into satin fill-in stitch on the trunk. You can use a cotton or polycotton on both top and bobbin for a nice bark texture. If you use different colours, the bobbin colours can be brought up onto the edge of the satin fill-in stitches, giving a more natural effect. This is done by tightening the top tension. If the top thread breaks, it is too tight and should be loosened slightly. By varying the tension the bobbin colour can be brought up and then let down, appearing and disappearing as you wish.

The branches are covered in a similar way. Pull the thick threads tightly as you wrap them in the cord method. You won't need to go to the ends of the branches. When the skeleton is attached, these ends can be extended on to the background and held there with embroidery.

The background, whether painted, embroidered or overlaid, should be in a hoop, stretched in the usual way. The tree is placed in position, branches and roots spread realistically and held by pins before being secured with tiny stitches and trimmed. The tree skeleton is then embroidered over, camouflaging the ends of the branches with extended branches and leaves. The thick threads give a roundness and nearness to the tree.

Free zig-zag and satin fill-in are used to cover or partially cover the underlying thick threads. Leaves and grasses, bushes, flowers, soil and pebbles realistically camouflage the roots. *Twin Trees at Leura* (page 63) was embroidered using all these techniques, as was the picture *Here I Am* (page 64). The foreground tree on the left of this picture was built up over a tree skeleton of thick cotton threads. Free zig-zag and satin fill-in covered the skeleton, making the tree stand out from the background and appear closer. The background was painted and embroidered first. The background fabric being heavy-duty calico, it was able to take the strain of the elaborate embroidery.

The picture on page 80, *Sunrise Over the Ocean*, also uses this technique for the silhouetted Norfolk Island pine tree. Its unusual leaves were embroidered with free-running and whip stitch. Look back to the tree and leaf exercise on page 38 for this technique.

Opposite page:
Twin Trees at Leura
(20 × 30 cm)

Tree skeleton exercises.

Above, the prepared tree skeleton ready for attachment to the background.

Below, tree skeletons can be prepared from thick cotton or linen threads

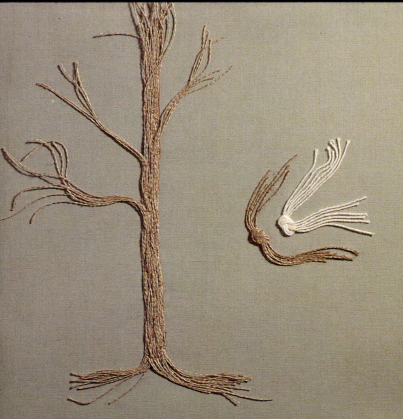

Here I Am (31 × 18 cm)

7 OVERLAYS AND UNDERLAYS

Early One Morning (12 × 20 cm)

Underwater scenes, caves, fogs and mists, rain, sunsets and sunrises, cloudy days, fireworks displays, leaves, silhouettes, special effects—and I'm sure you can think of many more—all lend themselves to the use of layers of coloured organza (both polyester and silk) or other semi-transparent fabrics.

Choose colour combinations to suit the mood of your picture. Try the colours under and then over each other—it is quite amazing how they can alter. Even the slight waterwave in the combination of the fabrics can add something to

a picture. One, two or three layers are generally enough, used over an opaque backdrop fabric that enhances their colours. Experiment again! The backdrop can be painted, as can one or each of the semi-transparent layers. Use a suitable paint for the particular fabric—Permaset for a cotton backdrop, Pebeo Setacolor Transparent for silk and polyester. (Refer to Chapter 8, Painting Backgrounds.)

Each layer, including the backdrop, can also be individually embroidered. They will need to be coordinated as they are placed over each other to create the depth and mood you are aiming for. I work with the layers in separate hoops, carefully placing one over the other to make sure that a particular subject will not be covered—or, conversely, to allow part of some foliage, for instance, to appear to grow from behind a rock. Separate fabric shapes can be appliquéd to the layers, either in front of or to the underside of the organza, and embroidered over. Your subject will dictate suitable fabrics—cotton, velvet, felt or leather for rocks, organza for wavy underwater reeds, for example. *Underwater Garden*, which also appears opposite the title page at the beginning of the book, illustrates some of these techniques. Even though some of the embroidery will be less visible in this haze you are creating, it will give your pictures distance and depth. Don't be afraid to experiment to develop your ideas.

Opposite page:
Underwater Garden (oval 16 × 21 cm)

Sea garden exercise

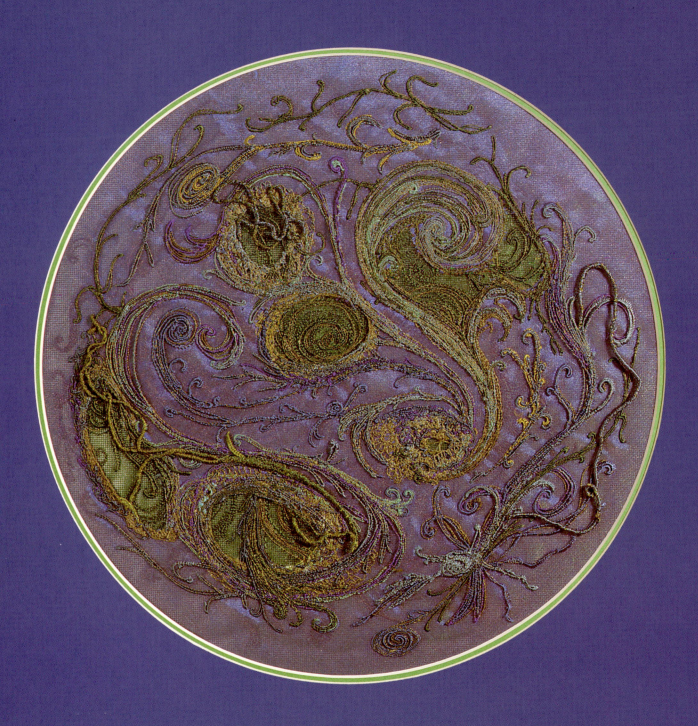

Whip stitch and feather stitch with rayon threads on both top and bobbin work very well on organza and similar fabrics. You will need to use a finer needle than for a calico background; size 80 is good for this combination. With the top tension slightly loose to normal, and the bobbin tension looser than normal, try out different effects on a piece of organza in a practice hoop. By using threads of different colours on top and in the bobbin, and by altering top tension a little at a time to just bring up the lower colour, or loosening it to make it disappear, you can alternate between the two colours. Try also a small width zig-zag, working the machine faster than normal and your hoop slowly and smoothly.

Although feather stitch is generally recommended as a circular motion stitch, great textural effects are possible by using it just going back and forth in any direction, straight or in a curve, sometimes using a tiny width zig-zag. Special care has to be taken, however, when working on any fine fabric. Doubling back in this back and forth method can cause tiny holes to appear in the fabric. To avoid this, go very slowly to the end of the line, stop, place the needle into the fabric, then carefully start again in the opposite direction. Practise this technique in your practice hoop first, using the same fabric as your picture. It is very important to begin and end with tiny stitches, as all the tension is on the top thread, and so extra care needs to be taken not to lose any of your embroidery.

Waterfalls, icicles, clothing and drapery, abstract designs, foliage and branches are but a few of many other good subjects for this method. They can be embroidered into the picture itself, into the layers or onto separate pieces added later using appliqué.

Twin Trees at Leura, on page 63, has a painted and then embroidered backdrop of heavy-duty calico. A sky was painted on organza, and applied to the embroidered background, with more embroidery over the two layers for the near part of the scene. With such a large expanse of sky the painted polyester organza softened the coarseness of the painted calico, and gave a misty effect over the far distant mountains. The tree trunks and branches are of wrapped linen threads, applied with embroidered leaves to the misty background.

A similar technique is used for the sunrise in *Sunrise Over the Ocean* on page 80. The sunrise, again painted on polyester organza, was coordinated with the painting on the heavy-duty calico, giving a softness of colour and depth. It is quite surprising to see how transparent a piece of organza becomes when painted with similar colours to the backdrop, and how the night clouds and early morning colours come to life.

Early One Morning (page 66) also uses this technique. The sunrise was painted first on heavy-duty calico. The silk organza was painted to coordinate with the colours on the backdrop. The organza overlay was embroidered with charcoal and black cotton threads to create silhouettes of the trees and bushes as seen from the window. The window is represented by a border. Free zig-zag, whip stitch, feather stitch and free-running were used for the embroidery.

The picture on page 68 shows an underwater scene in progress. The crystal blue organza, still in the hoop, has been embroidered with a matching cotton thread on top. Many colours of rayon thread were used on the bobbins. The top and bobbin tensions were adjusted for whip stitch and feather stitch. Deep textures were formed on the organza by moving the hoop very slowly, thus allowing the rayon threads to build up.

A Canopy of Kelp uses two layers of silk organza. The top layer is blue, the under layer green. The silvery fabric used for the backdrop gives a watery sheen to the picture. The organza layers were embroidered separately with whip and feather stitches, using rayon threads. Holes cut in the top layer to expose the underlay were embroidered around and over using openwork lace. Wrapped threads come up from these areas and lie across the top of the kelp canopy. Some of these have been attached using applied thread techniques, others are held invisibly with tiny stitches done by hand.

Layered Leaves (page 72) is a combination of shadow appliqué, quilting and free-machine embroidery. First, a background of black cotton fabric was placed over some thin wadding and backed with a fine cotton muslin to hold the wadding when quilted. The resulting sandwich was then basted together.

The leaves were cut out of silk organza of various colours, using paper templates, and placed decoratively, with some overlapping, onto the background. A piece of black organza was then placed carefully over the leaves. Pins were used to hold all in place, and were removed after basting.

Because of the thickness of this work, no hoop

Opposite page:

A Canopy of Kelp (25 cm diameter)

Layered Leaves

was necessary, but it was necessary to use the darning foot or the free-machine embroidery foot, and to hold the work firmly at all times. A Metalfil needle was used for the gold metallic thread on top, working with a loosened tension. The bobbin was filled with a yellow cotton thread at a normal tension.

The embroidery was started from the centre (all good quilting begins there) and gradually worked out to the sides. The main veins were begun at the base of each leaf, using free-running, then doubled back on the same line. The leaves were outlined in free-running. The stalks were free zig-zag—which also neatened each leaf base.

Some irregular spots on the leaves were outlined with free-running. The black overlay of organza was delicately trimmed away on the inside of the spots, using sharp, very fine, pointed scissors. The coloured leaf underlay, now revealed, was embroidered decoratively around the outside of the spots, mainly on the overlay. Some of the leaves were embroidered with many veins to create a lacy pattern.

This technique can be used in a variety of ways, for example, on evening bags and jackets, clothing, cushions and other household items as well as on pictures.

8 PAINTING BACKGROUNDS

Being able to paint backgrounds for your embroidery is a great advantage. It gives your embroidery individuality—a uniqueness you can call your own. You can mix and paint the colours of your choice on fabrics that are suitable for both painting and free-machine embroidery. You do not need to paint a fully finished artist's picture (unless you want to, of course). Small patches and splotches of colour, from a nearly dry brush, are often enough to give depth to the textures of the embroidery.

It is important to begin with the far background—in a landscape or a seascape this would be the sky. A portrait or still life might have a curtain and maybe a window, or just a flat wall of colour. The background is painted first, and pressed when dry to set the paints. Subsequently the middle distance and closer parts are painted in turn, the closest being last.

I will discuss the painting of both cotton and silk backgrounds in this chapter.

The sky was painted first on this calico background for an embroidered tree. The trunk and branches, painted next, are merely guidelines—the embroidery will build up the texture of the bark. The leaves were painted with an almost dry stiff-bristled small brush (page 78)

Painting Cotton

Choose a firm, closely woven cotton. Heavy-duty calico or a fine canvas is suitable for both painting and embroidery. Always wash the fabric first to remove the sizing. When almost dry, press it so that it is ready for use. It is convenient to have prepared fabric always on hand for when inspiration or necessity demands.

You can use old hoops for painting, or buy the inexpensive versions. The cheap ones will do because the fabric doesn't have to be drum tight—just firm in the hoop. Ideally, hoops for painting should be slightly larger than your embroidery hoops to allow the painted area to extend past the edges of the area to be embroidered. The painting hoops can be covered with masking tape to protect their surfaces from paint. The tape can be wiped clean more easily than the wood, and can also be removed and replaced when necessary.

The fabric should be about 10 cm wider than the diameter of the painting hoop to allow for handling, and the later framing of the picture. The fabric should be placed uppermost in the painting hoop—that is, the other way around to free-machine embroidery. The fabric should be straight by the grain, firmly and evenly stretched (but not to drum-tightness), and the screw tightened to hold it.

Requirements for painting on cotton
• Hoops (two or more) 20–25 cm diameter, covered with masking tape.
• Permaset Fabric Printing Colour paints—at least red, yellow and blue. Many other colours can be mixed from these.

Painting requirements

Simple examples of mixing colours from basic red, yellow and blue—the results can be extended almost endlessly with the use of water to dilute and/or the addition of reducer to lessen a colour's intensity

- Permaset Reducer—this reduces the intensity of the colours without changing their consistency.
- Paint brushes of assorted thicknesses, some bristly, others firm (as shown in the photograph).
- Jar of water for rinsing the brushes.
- Small glass jars with screwtop lids for mixing and storing the paints.
- Palette for mixing the paints if you have no jars. (Small jars are better because surplus paint can be saved rather than rinsed away.)
- Bottle with a dropper for adding clean water to dilute the paints. It's much cleaner and more controlled than adding water with a brush.
- Palette knife (or paddle-pop sticks) to remove paint from the jars and for mixing.
- An old clean towel for use as a paint rag. Tissues are useful, too.
- A hair dryer for drying paintings quickly.
- An iron to set the paint when thoroughly dry.
- Two pressing cloths, one to protect the ironing board cover, the other to protect the painting while being heat set. (Check the manufacturer's instructions here.)
- A laundry spray bottle is useful for dampening fabrics.

Work through the following exercises, which are very quick to do. They will teach you control over diluted paints. Study the photographs of each example before you start.

Exercise 1—Flat-wash
Dampen the stretched fabric with clean water, using either a clean thick brush or a laundry spray bottle. Check that the fabric is evenly dampened by holding it up to the light. Mix the colour you have chosen with clean water to a thin consistency. (Test it on the outer edge of the framed fabric.) Make sure that there is enough paint for the whole area to be painted. Working quickly with a thick brush, paint across the dampened fabric from top to bottom.

Exercise 2—Diluting and controlling the paint
Working quickly with a thick paint brush, and starting at the top, paint one or two wide brush strokes across the top of the fabric. Quickly dilute the colour in the small jar or palette with a little clean water and apply to the fabric in the same way, just below the colour already on the fabric, and let them run into each other. Dilute yet again and paint on in the same way.

A flat-wash. The damp fabric was painted with the same strength of colour all over

A diluted wash. The dampened fabric was painted with progressively diluted bands of the same colour

Merging of colours on a damp background

Merging of colours on a dry background is minimal

Exercise 3—Merging colours

Prepare three colours by diluting them with water—mix a double quantity. Prepare two hoops, dampening the fabric in one and leaving the other dry.

Paint one colour after the other, allowing the colours to run together on the dampened fabric, and then paint the dry fabric. Compare the difference. This exercise will give you experience for the next one.

Exercise 4—Sunrise

The photograph shows a sunrise painted on heavy calico. An overlay of similarly painted silk organza covers half of the calico, showing how the organza can soften its appearance.

Paint a sunset or sunrise of your own.

Any surplus paint on your painting can be absorbed with a clean damp brush, squeezed out first on the paint rag. Allow the painting to dry. You can speed up the process with the hair dryer.

When the paint is completely dry, press on the wrong side for about a minute to set the paint, using the iron at the correct temperature for the fabric you are working on. The fabric should then be pressed on the right side under a clean cloth for another minute. Check with the manufacturer's instructions for details.

When you paint a subject onto a prepared, painted and pressed background you would not generally use watery paints. For this part of the painting mix Reducer with the colours to be used—some water, too, if necessary, but only drop by drop. If the paints are too watery they will run into the painted background, leaving an uncontrolled, bleeding edge. Keep your brushes clean, but damp, not wet, when going into the paint.

In the example of a tree on a pre-painted blue sky background, which opens this chapter (page 75), the trunk and branches were painted first, being little more than guide lines for the embroidery, which will build up the texture of the bark. The leaves were painted with an almost dry, stiff-bristled small paint brush. The autumn colours, previously mixed using a small amount of Reducer, were dotted onto the background, the colours intermingled to look realistic. The embroidered picture will allow most of these colours to show behind the texture of the embroidered leaves, giving dimension and depth.

This technique has been used in most of my painted and embroidered pictures. Look at *Scorched Trees I* and *II* (pages 26 and 56), and at *At Coogee*

Ladies (page 96); *Sea Lace* (page 37) and *Here I Am* (page 64) also use the technique. You will recognise it if you look closely.

The photograph on the lower right shows embroidered and painted flowers on a painted yellow background. A flat-wash was applied first to the heavy-duty calico. The anemones were painted with brightly-coloured mixed paints thinned only with Reducer. For comparison, I have embroidered only part of the picture. Firstly, this shows you a very simple painting—it doesn't have to be elaborate, because the embroidery makes it elaborate. Secondly, by using the stitches effectively the painting is enlivened with details and textures.

Painting Your Own Picture

When you are ready to begin painting have on display the drawing, design or snapshots of what you are going to paint. Any research that you have done should be on hand too.

Outline your subject on to the fabric carefully. This can be done in various ways:

• Painting directly onto the fabric.
• Drawing the outline carefully first with a very sharply pointed hard pencil. These lines *must* be camouflaged with the painting or the embroidery.
• Marking around a template or a stencil, using the hard pencil method.
• Tracing your picture from the original onto some tissue paper. Pin the paper underside up on to the wrong (underside) of the fabric. (If you can't see the tracing, go over it with a pencil on the untraced side.) Place the fabric with the pinned tracing into your embroidery hoop in the usual way and with free-running stitches outline the tracing. The tissue paper can then be removed carefully (remove all the bits and pieces). The design will now be stitched through to the right side of the fabric, ready for painting. This stitching must be hidden by the embroidery (or unpicked later).

Start by painting the background, and go on from there. When you mix up your paints, always make more than you think you will need. Having to stop midway to mix more paint is not a good idea. Any paint left over can be kept in the little screwtop jars.

Sunrise painted on heavy calico, the right half overlaid with silk organza painted similarly

Anemones painted and partially embroidered

Sunrise Over the Ocean (19 × 25 cm)

Painting Silk

Pure silk fabrics painted with special paints can create beautiful backgrounds for embroideries. The colours are transparent and combined with the lustre of the silk can create some lovely effects.

There are many paints available for painting on silk. I have found Pebeo Setacolor Transparent paints to work very well. They can be used straight from the bottle and can also be diluted with water. The colours are good and mix together easily. When the painting is dry the colours are simply heat-set with an iron.

Silk was sprinkled with salt while still wet, causing the colours to migrate in interesting patterns. The fabric has been worked with openwork techniques, and quilted

Because silk is so fine, only light-weight embroideries should be planned. Silk quilts very well, which could be a consideration when designing a picture. Lightly padded quilting can give an added dimension and takes more embroidery than the silk alone.

Silk organza can be painted in the same way as silk, but with different results and for different purposes. The organza can be used as an overlay. This is especially useful when a heavy embroidery is planned, which of necessity must be on thick calico or canvas. Overlays can be used to counteract the coarseness of the background fabric. Look back at page 79, where a sunrise was painted on heavy-duty calico. A coordinated painting on silk organza covers half the calico, demonstrating its softening effect.

This same technique was used to soften the heavy calico background in *Impressions of Jenolan Caves* on page 91. I also used it for the sky and mountains behind the *Twin Trees at Leura* (page 63). *Sunrise Over the Ocean* (page 80) and *Early One Morning* (page 66) also use this technique.

Silk organza over silk induces a waterwave. For underwater scenes this adds to the enchantment. The opaque silk should be painted first, with enough colours mixed and ready for the organza overlay. Using two hoops, the overlay can be held over the underlay, and painted to coordinate.

Silk and organza can be sprinkled with coarse salt while the paint is still wet. The salt causes the colours to migrate, forming watery patterns and unusual designs. It is quite fascinating to watch this happening. The finished silk can be used for quilting. In the example of quilted silk on page 81, openwork techniques have also been used.

Requirements for painting on silk
Many of the requirements are the same as for painting on cotton, so check that you aren't doubling up unnecessarily.
• Hoops (two or more) 20–25 cm diameter, covered with masking tape.
• Pebeo Setacolor Transparent paints for fabrics—at least red, yellow and blue.
• Paint brushes—assorted thick, soft ones.
• Jar of water for rinsing the brushes.
• Bottle with a dropper for diluting the paints.
• Small glass jars with screwtop lids for mixing and storing the paints.
• Palette for mixing the colours if you prefer not to use the jars and lids.
• Palette knife (or paddle-pop sticks) for removing the paints and mixing them.

• Iron for setting the paints.
• Two pressing cloths, one to protect the ironing board cover, the other to protect the iron from salt and paint.
• Coarse salt (the type used for pickling). Other grades of salt can be used, giving different results.
• Plastic sheeting to go under the silk when using the salt technique. It should be slightly larger than the silk.
• Towel for squeezing dry the wet silk.
• Old towel for a paint rag.
• Polystyrene box for special effects using the salt technique. Thick white fruit-boxes of expanded polystyrene are available from greengrocers on request. Trim off the top rim, using a fine saw or a bread-knife if it is uneven, or if the box is too deep: 8–10 cm is deep enough, measured on the outside. Cover the edge with masking tape, which holds pins more securely than the polystyrene. Cover the inside of the box with stick-on plastic to prevent liquids trickling out of the holes in the bottom. This also makes the box much easier to keep clean.

All fabrics should be washed before painting. Pure silk is no exception, although it is possible to buy silk that is ready to paint without washing. This should be checked and confirmed by your supplier. If in doubt, wash it.

A word of warning here: the first and second exercises involve the salt technique. If the weather is very humid or very wet, leave them for another day. The salt attracts moisture from the air as well as the wet paint from the silk. This technique doesn't work well under humid conditions, and you will be left with the silk sitting in a solution of brine!

Exercise 1
Lay the piece of plastic sheeting on a smooth flat surface. Prepare the Setacolor paints by mixing colours, and diluting them with a little water. Try the colour on a small test piece of the silk you will be working on. Dampen the silk—if it gets too wet squeeze it in the towel. The silk should then be put onto the plastic. You can make little hills and valleys by gently pulling up parts of the silk here and there, or you may prefer to keep it quite flat.

Using a thick soft paint brush, place blobs of colour on to the dampened silk. Allow the colours to intermingle and run into each other. Any blank spaces can be left that way if you like.

Sprinkle the silk with the dry coarse salt. The migrating colours will run to the salt, up and down the contours of the silk. Leave the silk to dry at room

This collection of silk painting requirements includes a piece of silk suspended over a polystyrene box and treated with salt (Exercise 2)

Underwater painting (Exercise 4), painted silk organza layered over painted silk

temperature while the patterns are forming. When the salt is dry, brush it off the silk. (The salt can be collected, dried in a warm oven, and used again, providing it has not become too coloured.)

Press the silk between two cloths with the iron set at the correct temperature for silk. Follow the paint manufacturer's instructions.

If a powdered residue of salt is evident on the silk, wash it out in cool water. It can then be towel squeezed and pressed again when almost dry.

Exercise 2
Suspend a piece of dampened silk over the fruit-box, using pins to hold it by the four corners. Mix and dilute the paints you want to use. Paint a wide border of colour around the edges of the silk, encouraging

the paint to run slowly towards the centre. Sprinkle the painted area with the dry coarse salt.

The silk and salt should dry slowly. You will see shapes forming in a more organised manner than in the first exercise, gravitating towards the centre.

When dry, brush off the salt and follow the same ironing procedure as before to set the colours.

Silk organza can also be treated this way.

Exercise 3

Position a piece of silk organza in a painting hoop. (Always treat organza gently because there is a danger of 'bruising' such fine fabric.) Paint a sunrise to coordinate with the one you did on the calico background (page 79). When it is dry heat-set the painting between two cloths as usual.

I hope you will be inspired to go on and make a picture from your achievement.

Exercise 4

Use two painting hoops, putting a piece of silk in one and a piece of silk organza in the other. Make an underwater background, first on the opaque silk, then on the silk organza. Make sure to mix up enough paint for both, and coordinate the colours on the organza with those on the silk when painting it. Heat-set the dried work, as usual.

This can be the beginning of another picture. The photograph on the opposite page shows the finished fabrics, with the organza in the embroidery hoop.

After the Painting

Embroidering your own painted backgrounds is very satisfying. I always find it best to start embroidering with the background and then to come forward in imaginary layers, as on a stage setting. In the case of a landscape the already painted sky is usually best left alone, though that is a matter of personal choice. Start with the horizon, working on the distant shapes as they appear to you. Colours play a large part in establishing perspective and dimension, colours in the distance being muted and often hazy, and becoming clearer and more defined the nearer they are, as do the outlines. The imaginary layers can overlap each other, giving a three-dimensional effect, becoming more defined, more detailed, in clearer, more accurate colours. Various pieces of separately embroidered fabrics can be appliquéd for added detail and dimension and worked into the embroidery's second and front rows. Stumpwork pieces can also be incorporated. Separately made pieces to protrude from the picture can be created using fabric sculpting techniques, e.g. leaves and flowers.

In the case of portrait and still life pictures it is again preferable to embroider the background first, the background embroidery being brought very fractionally over the edge of the subject outline to avoid unworked areas. When the subject is embroidered it will then very slightly overlap the background, thus regaining its original outline and making a defined edge. This detail is visible in the picture *With Apologies to Vincent* (page 31).

Large flowers on still life pictures can be outlined around the edges of the painting, perhaps with their veins picked out. Stamens and other details can be defined using free-running, whip stitch or satin stitch as appropriate. Flowers can also be fully embroidered with free-running and satin fill-in. Use directional stitches, 'bleeding in' colours for light, shade, and contrasting colours as required. Look back at the pansy on page 24.

The painting can be completely covered with embroidery, as on a tapestry, or selected parts can be embroidered, coordinating with the painting. The embroidery will give textures and shape to the painting, which in turn gives depth and colour. Remember also that you can always add—it is very hard to unpick free-machine embroidery. Thought needs to be applied to this 'spontaneous' skill, so if you are in doubt try it out on a practice hoop first.

You can also create perspective with stitches; with a seascape the far distant sea up to the horizon can be worked in small free-running stitches; as it becomes nearer use slightly larger stitches; nearer still, free zig-zag. Then move to a very open satin fill-in. Leave spaces of painted fabric showing through to give a realistic effect. *Sea Lace* (page 37) and *Sunrise Over the Ocean* (page 80) both illustrate this technique.

Directions are very important to create mood and movement. Make the stitches work for you with their size, textures and colour. The exercise on page 88 shows two trees of the same colour, height and shape. The one on the left has been embroidered completely with free-running. The other tree has been embroidered with free zig-zag and satin stitch; you can see the roundness and shape that these stitches give, making the tree appear to be nearer.

The chart on pages 86–87, a guide only, suggests at a glance the various stitches and techniques you

Guide to Creating Distance, Depth and Dimension

Distance	Fabrics	Techniques
Sky and underwater	Heavy duty calico or similar, with optional overlays of organza	Painted Painted to coordinate
	Silk for light-weight embroideries with optional overlays of organza	Painted Painted to coordinate
Horizon— Landscapes Seascapes	As above	Painted
	Cotton, silk, satin, etc.	Appliquéd
	Thin wadding with a fine cotton backing	Quilted
Back Row	Optional layer of organza	Painted Embroidered Appliquéd
	Background to be backed with a fine cotton fabric	Trapunto quilting
Middle Row	Even-weave linen	Drawn thread work with openwork techniques
	Butter muslin	Pulled thread work Textures Embroidered appliqué
Front Row	Even-weave linen, cotton, velvet, organza, silk, georgette, felt, leather	Drawn thread and openwork Applied threads Painted and/or embroidered pieces Stumpwork Fabric sculpting

Note: The divisions do not run straight across the table because finite breaks between the divisions do not occur in reality — each area blends into the next.

Stitches	Colour and Shape
Sky—nil (or tiny free-running) Underwater: Whip stitch Feather stitch	True to life
Small free-running, small zig-zag	True to life
Underwater: feather stitch Small free running, free zig-zag, free satin stitch, whip stitch	Hazy and muted colours, undefined outlines, small distant shapes
Free satin stitch, satin fill-in, whip stitch, feather stitch	Becoming clearer, shapes in focus, slightly larger
Free zig-zag, satin fill-in, whip stitch, feather stitch	Clearest colours, largest shapes, very much in focus

Movement towards the viewer is suggested by the tree on the right, embroidered with free zig-zag and satin stitch; the tree on the left, embroidered in free-running, has far less impact

can use to create impressions of proximity and distance.

Landscapes can incorporate free-running to free zig-zag for treetops, getting larger and more detailed and defined in stitches and colours. Leave the painted colours showing through behind for depth, the stitches giving dimension and texture.

The picture *A Quiet Place* on page 39 shows how grasses can be embroidered with plenty of directions using free-running, whip stitch and zig-zag. A cotton or polyester thread on the top and a rayon thread in another shade or colour in the bobbin give a more natural look.

Floral gardens need plenty of colours in varying shades. Satin fill-in, whip stitch, feather stitch, zig-zag and free-running are all suitable for flowers and leaves. Your own knowledge and imagination will tell you when to use a particular stitch.

Threads that work with your subject are the ones to choose. The shiny rayon threads are good for watery, shiny, delicate fill-in subjects, whereas the coarser threads of cotton and polyester go very well with tree trunks, leaves, textures and bolder subjects (although sometimes to get a particular colour one has to be flexible). Thick threads can be applied freely to the fabric, both decoratively and usefully. They can be worked over to build up particular areas.

The embroidery artist must have the knowledge, ability and imagination to make a fabric painting come to life. Embroidery can create wonderful textures, and gives distance, depth and dimension to an otherwise flat painting.

9 STUMPWORK

Stumpwork is very similar to padded appliqué. Pieces are made separately, decorated and detailed with embroidery, padded, and then applied to the background embroidery. These pieces of raised embroidery give a three-dimensional appearance to the picture.

Cardboard is generally used as a base for this kind of work. Thin card, about postcard thickness, is ideal. This is covered with a layer of either thin wadding or felt. Sometimes both are used for greater thickness. The fabric previously embroidered, or left plain to be detailed later, becomes the top layer. There must be sufficient border around the fabric to allow it to be pulled over the layers of padding onto the back of the card shape. It is then laced from one side to the other with cotton thread. You mould and shape it as you progress—pulling it in more, or releasing it, to achieve the desired effect.

Before cutting out a shape, however, you need to know which way the grain of the card runs. To find this out, fold the card down one way, and then at right angles. You will find that one of the folds has less resistance and folds over in a straighter line than the other. This is the grain line. Another way to check is by tearing. Tear a thin strip down one side, and then again at right angles. The clean tear indicates the grain, the jagged one runs across it. The piece of torn cardboard in the picture on page 92 illustrates the difference.

You can use the grain to advantage with stumpwork as knowing it allows you to bend the card more readily. For instance, when making a human figure the grain line would generally run the length of the body. A short, fat figure could have the grain running across the body.

To make a first practice piece, choose a shape with a fairly smooth outline—perhaps a piece of fruit such as the pear in the photograph. I painted a small piece of silk for this one. Coloured silk, organza or fine cotton are also suitable. The colour of the semi-transparent organza or silk may be influenced by the felt underlay, which can give an interesting effect, and lead to more realistic results.

Draw your shape onto the card, with the grain in the best direction for your subject. The pear has the grain lengthways. Cut out the shape accurately and neatly.

Using the shape as a template, draw around it, making two more outlines on a piece of paper. Mark a line 3 mm on the inside of one of the outlines, making it smaller. This will be the pattern for the wadding. Mark a line 10 mm outside the other outline, making it larger. This pattern is for the fabric. Make a note to yourself on this pattern to mark out the fabric on the bias, which will allow neater shaping. The fabric should not be cut until after it has been painted and/or embroidered, nor should it be cut before you have machined a stay stitch around it.

Opposite page:
Impressions of Jenolan Caves *(23 × 38 cm)*

The stages in making the stumpwork pear, clockwise from top left: establishing the grain of the card and cutting the template, glueing the felt over the trimmed wadding already fixed to the card, the stretched and shaped silk top layer, and the laced back

Hooped organza showing the stitch lines for a stumpwork shell

Look at the photograph of the shell outline on organza in a small hoop. The shell shape has been outlined in free-running. The embroidery should extend about 3 mm past this first outline all around to allow for the thickness and roundness of the padding. The further outline, also in free-running, is needed to hold the lacing in the final stages. When cutting the fabric away after the embroidery has been completed, make certain to cut on the outside of this stitch line.

Going back to the pear, use a good quality craft glue to stick the wadding onto the card shape. Trim the wadding, holding the scissors at an angle to bevel the edges. Make sure that there is a border of 2–3 mm of card for the felt to be stuck onto. Cut a rough shape from the felt, larger than the card. Squeeze a thin line of craft glue on the perimeter of the card. Mould the felt over the wadding, gently shaping the card at the same time. Press the felt onto the card to stick it down. Hold it there for a few moments until it sticks properly. The felt can then be trimmed in line with the card.

As there was no embroidery on my pear example, only the outer stitchline of free-running was necessary on the fabric. The pear was cut out carefully on the outside of the stitching. A row of hand-running

Stages in creating the stumpwork shell

stitches on the inside of the machine stitching will ensure an even pull on the covering fabric. Use a double thickness of thread. Fit the fabric to the padded card, covering the padding evenly and pulling in the gathers made by the hand stitching. Secure this when you are satisfied with the result. With more double thread in your needle, lace the edges from opposite sides, moulding the shape as you go, pulling or releasing as you progress. You can see how this is done on both the pear and the next example, the shell.

The pear had wrapped linen threads added for its stalk. A small indentation was quilted to imply the flower end. A basket or bowl of fruit using this technique would look very appetising.

The shell was made in the same way as the pear, the main difference being that the outer fabric was fully embroidered. This was done using graduating widths of free zig-zag and satin fill-in. Free-running was used to give the bands of colour, and went right over the existing embroidery. Rayon threads were used on the top, and cotton threads on the bobbin.

The padding was slightly different. The wadding ended in a point so that the angular 'stem' of the shell could remain flat. The felt was stuck down onto this part of the card, giving the shell realistic contours. The embroidered fabric was quilted invisibly through the padded card to emphasise the V shape.

Impressions of Jenolan Caves, which opens this chapter (page 91), incorporates stumpwork techniques. The three stalagmites in the front of the picture stand out from the embroidered ones further back, creating a three-dimensional effect. They were made from organza, embroidered on the bias with whip stitch, free zig-zag and feather stitch. The card uses the grain vertically, and in this case was padded

with felt only. The pieces were encouraged into roundness by first moulding the padded card and then holding the shape with lacing. They were sewn onto the picture with invisible stitches.

The next picture, *At Coogee Ladies'*, also incorporates stumpwork techniques. The three women in the front were made from painted cotton fabric, cut on the bias. The felt padding on the card was doubled in parts—the reclining lady's breasts and hips had extra pieces added over the main piece of felt. The fat lady had extra pieces of felt placed under

Stumpwork stalagmite showing the technique used to form the stalagmites in Impressions of Jenolan Caves *(page 91)*

At Coogee Ladies' (29 × 23 cm)

the main body of felt. The grain of the card for her went across the body.

Separate heads were made for all the women, and attached invisibly afterwards. A separate arm and leg were necessary for the fat lady, and for the reclining lady in the centre. Quilting stitches, added here and there, went through all thicknesses. Hair made from stranded embroidery threads was couched, and then tied with a narrow ribbon. Hand-embroidered details—features and a needle-lace hat—were added.

The figures, now complete, were hand stitched to their beach towels. These had already been machine appliquéd to the hand-painted and free-machine embroidered background.

The three women further back were raised using Trapunto techniques. To do this the painted background had a piece of fine cotton muslin basted to it prior to the embroidery. The figures consist simply of an outline of free-running. After the background was embroidered through both thicknesses of fabric, the figures were padded through the cotton muslin. A small opening was made, and minute amounts of toy filling were pushed through, using a smoothed and rounded satay stick. This gave the figures a three-dimensional appearance that was less than that of the stumpwork figures in the front, and in keeping with the distance.

Hats, hair, towels, beachbags and thongs were added last of all, using hand embroidery techniques.

The background was of free-machine embroidery

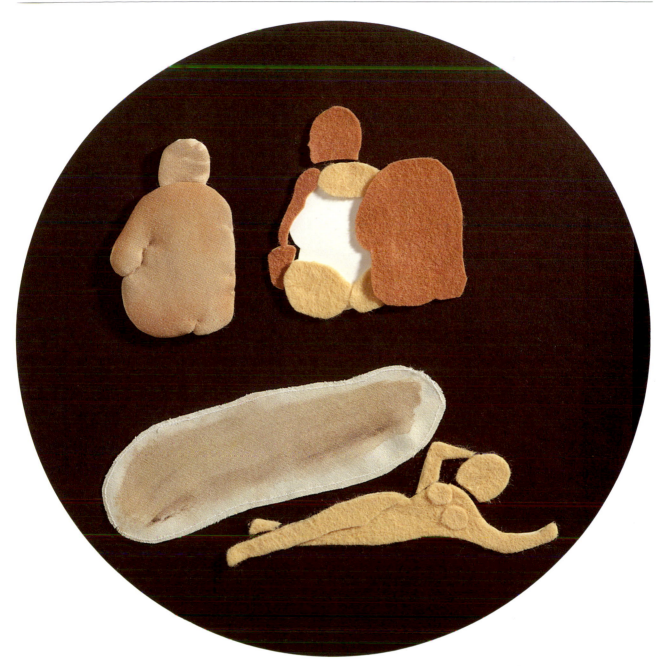

Building up the stumpwork figures for the picture opposite

using free-running, free zig-zag and whip stitch. The threads were mainly cotton and polycotton. The background fabric was heavy-duty calico, painted with fabric paints.

Even though the technique of stumpwork is centuries old, I find it very compatible with free-machine embroidery, with its ability to create further dimensions and depth.

Note—Coogee Ladies' Swimming Baths had a secluded but dilapidated area exclusively for nude women to take in the sunshine.

10 FABRIC SCULPTING

Fabric sculpting breaks all the rules! The fabric is pulled in with stitchery, allowing it to pucker and take on another shape. Generally no hoop is used. The fabric is moulded and formed by your hands.

Separate pieces are made and attached to the picture, usually with embroidery.

Impressions of the Imperial Cave
(oval 21 × 12 cm)

The pieces are quite formative, and give a soft three-dimensional quality to the picture. Whereas stumpwork is firm and finished when attached, these pieces are pliable, and can be shaped at the time of application.

You will need to use the free-machine embroidery foot if you have one, or the darning foot, as you need to protect your fingers from the needle. The feed-dog is lowered (or covered) as usual.

The fabric is worked on the bias. Silk organza responds very well. Plain silk and georgette also work well with this technique. The fabrics can be painted first if you wish.

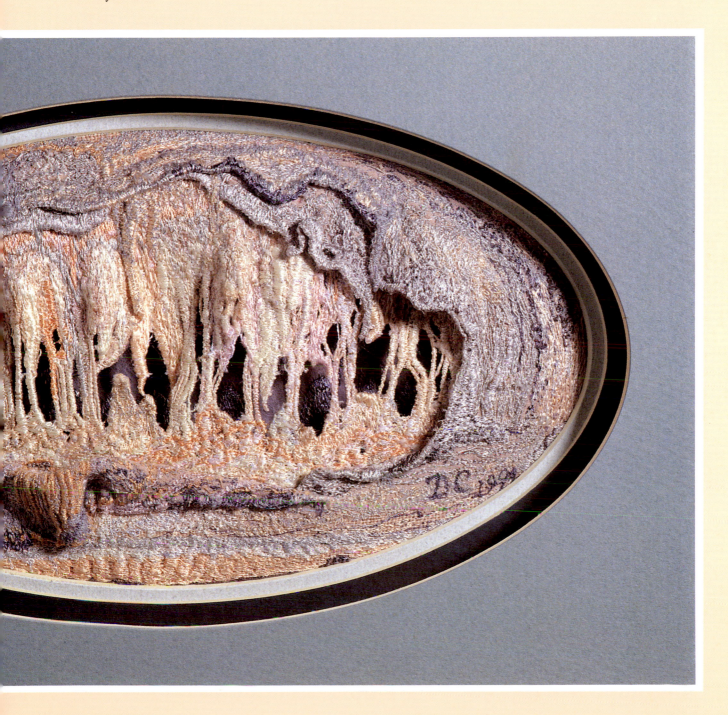

Fabric sculpting on silk organza

Fabric sculpting on silk

To practice, start with a square of organza, about 15 × 15 cm. Fold the square diagonally in half. The fold becomes the long edge of the piece. Because this is the bias line it will give and take more readily.

The fabric is held with both hands at the ends of the diagonal. It can also be held from the fold and the square corner to give another emphasis to the shaping.

The threads to use are cotton or polycotton, in conjunction with a silky rayon or a fine cotton. Various stitches and directions will influence the shaping of the fabric, and will dictate which thread to use on the top and in the bobbin.

The first picture shows circles and ovals worked with feather stitch on two pieces of silk organza. Cotton thread was used on top, with just enough tension to pull up the threads from below. The bobbin tension was quite loose. Fine cotton thread, rayon thread, and a very fine metallic thread were used on the bobbins, and came through decoratively. Notice how the top thread has pulled the circular directions of the stitches, forming small craters while moulding the fabric.

The next picture shows on the left a piece of silk, painted beforehand with leafy green colours. Whip stitch was used on this example, with cotton thread on the top. The bobbin held a rayon thread in a slightly loosened bobbin case. Circles, ovals, shells

Wisteria
Exercise in fabric sculpting

Surf exercises—heavily worked nylon net applied to a cotton background

and interlocking diamond shapes in the stitching pulled in the silk.

A similar piece was made for the leaf canopy of the wisteria on the previous page. It was then embroidered onto the background, leaving the lower edge free. Whip stitch and free zig-zag stitch were used to create more foliage, which disguised the join and extended the canopy.

The wisteria flowers were embroidered with whip stitch using mauves, pinks and purple rayon threads on the bobbin. The trunk was made from wrapped linen threads twisted around each other to look realistic. The ends were threaded through the background fabric and secured from behind.

The bottom photograph on page 100 also shows a piece of georgette, on the right. The shaping in this piece was encouraged by the use of free zig-zag and satin fill-in. The top thread is rayon, the tension normal to slightly loose. The bobbin thread is cotton, the tension normal to firm. You can see the initial directions of the free zig-zag stitches on the sample. They are gradually built up, intermingling to form satin fill-in. I used this technique on the outer edges of the picture *Impressions of the Imperial Cave.*

Suburban Waterfall

The water, garlands of feather stitch worked on silk organza, was applied to a lightly padded rayon fabric quilted to resemble a stone wall

The surf exercise opposite was begun on the hoop. The surf was embroidered on a single thickness of nylon net. Whip and feather stitches (used with a tiny width zig-zag) pulled in the net forming small holes and building up textures. It was then cut out, the lower edge neatened with free zig-zag and applied to the previously embroidered wave, which was composed of free-running and whip stitch. The directions of the stitches are well illustrated in this picture. The heavily embroidered net was arranged and attached only on the top with whip and feather stitches. The lower part of the surf was left loose to come forward to look like a breaking wave.

The suburban waterfall was also embroidered in the hoop. A single thickness of silk organza was worked on the bias. Garlands of feather stitch, overlapping and falling, were made to resemble the waterfall. Cotton thread was used on the top, and rayon threads on the bobbin.

The fabric was then cut larger than the embroidery

The construction process used in the 'wings' appearing at the top of Impressions of
Jenolan Caves *(page 90)*

to allow for turning and attachment. It was carefully draped, pinned and fitted to the wall, which was previously quilted on a lightly padded rayon fabric. Free-running circles and ovals were embroidered to look like stones. The waterfall was attached with free-running. Feather stitch was used to emulate the froth of the water at the base. Plants were embroidered using free-running and whip stitch.

The 'wings' at the top of the picture *Impressions of Jenolan Caves* (page 91) were sculpted from silk organza. First a long triangular shape was cut from paper. This pattern was pinned to the organza with the centre fold of the paper on the exact bias of the fabric.

The organza was then cut and folded and the two sides were seamed together. The technique is illustrated here, photographed step by step. The shape was then turned right side out, and pressed very lightly with the seam line underneath and in the centre.

Lengths of cotton, threaded double through a hand sewing needle, were attached to each end of the fabric and knotted. These were used to hold and manipulate the fabric, as the pieces are rather small.

The 'wing' could also be pulled sideways to make use of the bias in the opposite direction by attaching threads to the sides.

The 'wings' were embroidered mainly in an up and down direction using whip stitch and feather stitch. Sometimes a small zig-zag width was incorporated. Cotton thread was used on top with a tightened tension. The bobbins were filled with rayon threads of apricots and pinks and changed frequently. The tension was fairly loose so that a lovely rich texture appeared.

The holding threads can be removed by trimming and neatening if necessary with embroidery. Alternatively, they could be wrapped with free zig-zag, then folded back into the wing, secured and trimmed to become a part of the whole piece. Slits are also an option—and should be edged with free zig-zag.

When completed, the wings were placed, pushed into shape and pinned into position. They were then embroidered onto the picture, using free-running with matching threads.

11 INSPIRATIONS

Let me add just a few words about ideas and inspirations. Sometimes they are plentiful, other times not so easy to find. As soon as you have an idea, draw it, or write it down!

By keeping quick sketches and notes of your ideas, you will always be reminded of incidents, thoughts, people and places that have inspired you, however briefly. Take your camera as well as your sketch book on all outings and excursions. Sometimes a quick snapshot is all you will have time for.

Later, when you go through your ideas, you will become as enthusiastic as you were when you first recorded them. Having a collection of ideas is like having money in the bank, or food in the freezer!

Have these reminders and your research at hand while you plan your design, and also when you are ready to embroider. Imagine you are there with the subject. Think of it and make it become real and alive.

Don't be afraid to change your mind as your picture progresses. You are merely developing your idea. Quite often, new thoughts suggest themselves once you have begun. Don't shun them. Consider them and try them out. Sometimes they are better—if not, you are no worse off.

Keep experimenting, and trying out other ways. From every picture that I have made, a new idea or technique has developed. Make a note of what you do, and keep a sample of what has been tried for your reference book. Even if it wasn't suitable this time, next time you will be able to see where you were, and how to go on from there.

Free-machine embroidery is a creative and developing art that will grow with you.

I hope that you have enjoyed this book and will be able to use what you have learned as a basis to branch out into the direction that is *you*.

A collection of ideas...

APPENDIX

Personal Stitch Summary

Stitch	Tension		Stitch	
	Top	*Bobbin*	*Length*	*Width*

★ Normal refers to the normal techniques as used in dressmaking
★★ Always move the hoop smoothly

Date ....

Threads		Speed		Application
Top	*Bobbin*	*Machine*	*Hoop*★★	

INDEX

(Pictures are listed in *italic* type)